Kingdom First

Bible Studies
For the Kingdom -
New Covenant Church

Volume III

Stan Newton

Kingdom First
Bible Studies for the Kingdom -
New Covenant Church
By Dr. Stan Newton

© 2018 by Stan Newton

Endorsement from Solid Rock Church
Sedona, Arizona

Stan Newton's *Kingdom First* Bible course is a three-part scriptural exegesis with historical-contextual accuracy based on the "Dream of God!" The course takes you through to the fulfillment of His dream completing the circle of transformation with the student. The study covers the dream of God beginning in Genesis and takes people through to the revelation of the whole picture contained in the vision of the Father for mankind.

Solid Rock chose this study because we want our congregation to grow in greater understanding and knowledge of the better new covenant, kingdom, and eschatology. We have utilized this study in our church, using the discussion questions at the end of each chapter as a tool to apply the gospel of the Kingdom principles in the everyday life of a believer.

Patricia Garitson,
Kingdom Revivalist
Shapeyourdestinyimage.com
www.solidrockchurchofsedona.com

Table of Contents

Preface

Advancing the Reign of Christ through biblical education is the goal of *Kingdom First*. Audacious as it seems, I am convinced the 'renewing of the mind' through biblical understanding is key to bringing the church closer to its calling and mission from God. These lessons set the kingdom of God within time - our time and history. The kingdom is within and among us; it is our message and our guarantee that God is a covenant keeping God.

Within churches which embrace charismatic gifts there are tendencies to elevate experience over the study of Scripture. What is needed now is not the devaluing of our spiritual experiences but the raising of our level of understanding the word of God. Understanding how the kingdom of God works in Scripture will sharpen our calling, empower our mission, refocus the church, enhance discipleship and deepen our worship. It is time to see the kingdom of God placed where it belongs - as the central cord that unites the Bible. It is time to "Seek first the kingdom of God."

Kingdom First is presented in three volumes. The first begins with Genesis and takes us through the key Old Testament Scriptures about the kingdom. In Volume II we start with John the Baptist and study the birth, life, miracles and teachings of Jesus. We focus on His kingship and how He viewed the kingdom of God in His ministry. The final volume begins with the pouring out of the Holy Spirit and looks at the early church and how we are the heirs of those who advanced the kingdom of God in the earth.

For Teachers: *Kingdom First* is a teaching manual which does not go into detail on each subject. Therefore, if you are a teacher, I would advise that you read my two books, *Glorious Kingdom* and *Glorious Covenant*. Also, reading Jonathan Welton's *Understanding the Whole Bible* would be helpful. If students are not familiar with basic terms in eschatology or in the study of the covenants, a summary of terms may be needed before beginning. God is restoring key areas of Scripture in our generation to prepare the church to advance the kingdom of God. My prayer is that these lessons will help in that effort.

Stan Newton
Sofia, Bulgaria

Lesson 1
The Spirit Falls -
The Dream is Realized

What is our mission? What is the purpose of the church? When the Spirit came on the day of Pentecost, the mission was clarified. Even though 'God's Dream' got back on track when Jesus gave His life on a cross, it took a while for the people to recognize what happened. When the Holy Spirit fell, all doubts, confusion and uncertainty evaporated like a thin fog on a sunny morning. Their minds were renewed, and their spirits empowered. They knew Jesus was at the right hand of God and the kingdom was in session.

The Day of Pentecost was the eschatological fulfillment of the kingdom.

The gift of the Spirit changed everything!

Old Testament and the Holy Spirit

Contrary to what many believe, the Holy Spirit was active in the Old Testament. From Genesis to Malachi, we can find evidence of the Holy Spirit working in the lives of the people. In the New Testament, the authors normally use the term, 'Holy Spirit' or just the 'Spirit', whereas in the Old Testament, several different terms were used, while 'Holy Spirit' appears only three times (Ps.51:11, Is. 63:10-14 twice). The terms used in the Old Testament are, "Your Spirit," "The Spirit," "My Spirit," "The Spirit of the Lord," "The Spirit of judgment or fire," and "The Spirit of God."

The first reference to the Holy Spirit occurs in the creation account of Genesis.

Now the earth was formless and empty, darkness was over the surface of the deep, and the Spirit of God was hovering over the waters. (Genesis 1:2)

First this: God created the Heavens and Earth—all you see, all you don't see. Earth was a soup of nothingness, a bottomless emptiness, an inky blackness. God's Spirit brooded like a bird above the watery abyss. (The Message: Genesis 1:1-2)

The Message translation brings out several images which can evoke questions. "Why did God create a "Soup of nothingness," or a "Bottomless emptiness?"

Another question would be, "Why was the Holy Spirit brooding over this wasteland?" I'm not sure any of us can answer these questions will full assurance. There is an element of mystery in creation and maybe that is good. What we know for sure was the Holy Spirit was active in the creation.

The Work of the Holy Spirit in the Old Testament

1. **He was the source of life** (Genesis 1:2, Job 33:4).

2. **He was the source of creation and renewal** (Psalm 104:30).

3. **He was the source of Teaching** ((Nehemiah 9:20).

4. **He was the source that empowered the people of God** (I Chronicles 28:11-19).

Then David presented his son Solomon with the plans for The Temple complex: porch, storerooms, meeting rooms, and the place for atoning sacrifice.

He turned over the plans for everything that God's Spirit had brought to his mind: the design of the courtyards, the arrangements of rooms, and the closets for storing all the holy things. He gave him his plan for organizing the Levites and priests in their work of leading and ordering worship in the house of God, and for caring for the liturgical furnishings. He provided exact specifications for how much gold and silver was needed for each article used in the services of worship: the gold and silver Lampstands and lamps, the gold tables for consecrated bread, the silver tables, the gold forks, the bowls and the jars, and the Incense Altar. And he gave him the plan for sculpting the cherubs with their wings outstretched over the Chest of the Covenant of God—the cherubim throne. "Here are the blueprints for the whole project as God gave me to understand it," David said (1 Chronicles 28:11-19).

God spoke to Moses: "See what I've done; I've personally chosen Bezalel son of Uri, son of Hur of the tribe of Judah. I've filled him with the Spirit of God, giving him skill and know-how and expertise in every kind of craft to create designs and work in gold, silver, and bronze; to cut and set gemstones; to carve wood—he's an all-around craftsman (Exodus 31:1-5).

These passages about the work of the Holy Spirit are fascinating. Today, it seems like we ask for the Holy Spirit to fill us and give us 'spiritual gifts' but not usually the type of gifts we see in these passages. Should we be expecting more? Have we limited what the Holy Spirit can impart in our lives?

5. **He is the source or manifestation of the presence of God** (Psalms 139:7).

Prophecy concerning the Holy Spirit in the age of the Messiah (New Covenant)

> *For I will pour water on the thirsty land, and streams on the dry ground; I will pour my Spirit upon your offspring, and my blessing on your descendants And a Redeemer will come to Zion, to those in Jacob who turn from transgression," declares the Lord.* (Isaiah 44:3)

> *And as for me, this is my covenant with them," says the Lord: "My Spirit that is upon you, and my words that I have put in your mouth, shall not depart out of your mouth, or out of the mouth of your offspring, or out of the mouth of your children's offspring," says the Lord, "from this time forth and forevermore.* (Isaiah 59:20-21)

> *And when they come there, they will remove from it all its detestable things and all its abominations. And I will give them one heart, and a new spirit I will put within them. I will remove the heart of stone from their flesh and give them a heart of flesh, that they may walk in my statutes and keep my rules and obey them. And they shall be my people, and I will be their God.* (Ezekiel 11:18-20)

> *And it shall come to pass afterward, that I will pour out my Spirit on all flesh; your sons and your daughters shall prophesy, your old men shall dream dreams,*

and your young men shall see visions.
Even on the male and female servants
in those days I will pour out my Spirit. (Joel
2:28-29)

The Day of Pentecost

The Apostles were aware of the many prophecies from
the Old Testament about the Holy Spirit. Now, because of the
instructions from Jesus, they were praying and waiting for
something to happen. Jesus taught them about the coming of
the Spirit and what would occur, when He came.

Ask many Pentecostal/charismatic believers about the
purpose of 'Pentecost' and central in their thinking is the
Baptism in the Holy Spirit and speaking in tongues.
Complete denominations have been built around this
doctrine. Yet, as vital as the filling of the Spirit is, we must
connect the power of the Spirit not to 'speaking in tongues'
but to the arrival of God's kingdom on earth. Pentecost is all
about the kingdom!

With the cross and resurrection of Jesus now completed,
why must His followers wait?

Being Filled or Baptized?

Evangelical believers outside Pentecostal / Charismatic
churches tend to equate being filled with the Spirit as being
under the control of the Spirit. They do not see it as a
'spiritual experience', but as a lifelong process of
sanctification. On the Pentecostal / Charismatic side, being
filled or baptized in the Holy Spirit is a spiritual experience,
which occurs after our salvation. Therefore, all Evangelicals
teach we are to be filled with the Holy Spirit, but as to when
and how that happens, there is a huge difference.

Traditional Evangelicals believe we are filled at the time
of salvation, while Pentecostals teach there is a second work
of grace, where believers are Baptized in the Holy Spirit with
the evidence of speaking in tongues. Additionally, there are

leaders who are not part of historic Pentecostal churches, but have been involved in Charismatic churches, that teach any gift of the Spirit is the evidence, or possibly love is the evidence.

Traditional Pentecostal teaching insists on two doctrinal convictions.

> 1. Personal salvation (born again - saved) and the Baptism in the Holy Spirit are two separate events. We are first born again and then Baptized in the Holy Spirit.

> 2. Speaking in tongues is the evidence of being Baptized in the Holy Spirit.

The Assemblies of God denomination is a historic Pentecostal movement, which teaches the Baptism in the Holy Spirit must include speaking in tongues.

"Though many non-Pentecostals teach a baptism in the Holy Spirit without speaking in tongues, the position of the Assemblies of God is clearly declared in Section 8 of its Statement of Fundamental Truths: "The baptism of believers in the Holy Spirit is witnessed by the initial sign of speaking with other tongues, as the Spirit of God gives them utterance (Acts 2:4). The evidence always occurred (and still does today) at the time believers were baptized in the Spirit, not at some indeterminate future time."[1]

Biblical scholar J. Rodman Williams agrees that being saved and Baptized in the Holy Spirit are separate experiences.

"At the time of salvation, the Holy Spirit comes to dwell within. For example, the risen Christ breathed on the disciples and said, "Receive the Holy Spirit" (John 20:22). At Pentecost, there came about a later experience of the disciples being baptized in the Holy Spirit, primarily for ministry in the power of the Holy Spirit (Acts 1:5-8 and 2:4). Two separate experiences: one for enlivening by the Holy Spirit for salvation; the other for empowering by the Holy Spirit. We need both."[2]

Using Acts 2:4 as our starting point, we will trace instances, where the disciples of Jesus were filled with the Holy Spirit, after their experience on the day of Pentecost.

> *When the day of Pentecost came, they were all together in one place. Suddenly a sound like the blowing of a violent wind came from heaven and filled the whole house where they were sitting. They saw what seemed to be tongues of fire that separated and came to rest on each of them. All of them were filled with the Holy Spirit and began to speak in other tongues as the Spirit enabled them.* (Acts 2:1-4)

> *Then Peter, filled with the Holy Spirit, said to them: "Rulers and elders of the people!* (Acts 4:8)

> *And when they had prayed, the place in which they were gathered together was shaken, and they were all filled with the Holy Spirit and continued to speak the word of God with boldness.* (Acts 4:31)

In these two instances it is likely that both Peter and the assembled believers were filled with the Spirit in the present. The context would have us believe that Luke was not referring to the Day of Pentecost, but to a present experience. The place was shaken, and because of the 'Filling of the Holy Spirit" they spoke with boldness.

The Bible speaks of individuals and groups who were filled with the Holy Spirt and it was not limited to a single event. We can be filled many times. Yet, as we study the Scriptures, there is a single event, which precedes all fillings and it was called '*The Promise of the Father*' and '*The Gift of the Holy Spirit.*'

> *"And behold, I am sending the promise of my Father upon you. But stay in the city until you*

> *are clothed with power from on high."* (Luke 24:29)

> *And Peter said to them, "Repent and be baptized every one of you in the name of Jesus Christ for the forgiveness of your sins, and you will receive the gift of the Holy Spirit. For the promise is for you and for your children and for all who are far off, everyone whom the Lord our God calls to himself."* (Acts 2:38-39)

It is this the '*Promise of the Father*' and the '*Gift of the Holy Spirit*' that the followers of Jesus received on the day of Pentecost?

While Peter was preaching to a group of Gentiles the Holy Spirit fell.

> *While Peter was still saying these things, the Holy Spirit fell on all who heard the word. And the believers from among the circumcised who had come with Peter were amazed, because the gift of the Holy Spirit was poured out even on the Gentiles. For they were hearing them speaking in tongues and extolling God. Then Peter declared, "Can anyone withhold water for baptizing these people, who have received the Holy Spirit just as we have?" And he commanded them to be baptized in the name of Jesus Christ. Then they asked him to remain for some days.* (Acts 10:44-48)

Why was Peter convinced that God had fully accepted the gentiles? Because they were receiving the '*Gift of the Holy Spirit*', just like they did on the day of Pentecost; including speaking in tongues. The New Testament points to an original experience of receiving the '*Promise of the Father*', which is being 'Baptized in the Holy Spirit' and then all through our lives we can be 'filled' again and again with the Spirit.

We also can conclude that 'speaking in tongues' is a vital aspect of receiving this Baptism in the Spirit. It was because Peter heard the gentiles speaking in tongues that he knew God had accepted them.

One way we can clarify the difference between the indwelling Holy Spirit we receive at salvation and the 'Baptism in the Holy Spirit' we receive afterwards is the role taken by the Spirit or Jesus in each case.

> *For in one Spirit we were all baptized into one body—Jews or Greeks, slaves[d] or free—and all were made to drink of one Spirit.* (I Corinthians 12:13)

> *And John bore witness: "I saw the Spirit descend from heaven like a dove, and it remained on him. I myself did not know him, but he who sent me to baptize with water said to me, 'He on whom you see the Spirit descend and remain, this is he who baptizes with the Holy Spirit.'* (John 1:32-33)

In the Corinthian passage I see Apostle Paul stating that when anyone - Jew or Greek, slave or free - come to Christ, they are made equal, because the Holy Spirit is the One, who baptizes them in the body of Christ.

In John's passage it is Jesus doing the baptizing. The Ascended Christ, from His highly exalted position, is the One, who baptizes us in the Holy Spirit. First, at salvation, we are brought into (immersed) into the church, the body of Christ. Second, Jesus baptizes us into the Holy Spirit.

Over time and with better theological light there may be a better way to explain the ministry of receiving the '*gift of the Holy Spirit*'. Yet, because the church needs to move powerfully in the Holy Spirt and to manifest His gifts, it is not a time to water down the teaching which was restored in the Azusa Street revival.

Discussion and Questions

1. John 20:22 says of Jesus, "*He breathed on them and said to them, Receive the Holy Spirt.*" Why then did they need to wait to be filled on the Day of Pentecost?

2. What are your thoughts of the Spirit brooding over the creation? Is there any application to our lives in this work of the Spirit?

3. What was your experience with being 'filled' or 'Baptized' in the Holy Spirit? Was it a natural and easy path, or was it difficult because of prior teaching?

4. Why is the ministry of the Holy Spirit imperative to the advancing of the kingdom of God? We know the Spirt gives gifts to His people. Should we expect the Spirit to give natural gifts like in the Old Testament?

Footnotes

[1] https://ag.org/Beliefs/Topics-Index/Holy-Spirit-Baptism-Baptism-in-the-Holy-Spirit

[2] http://www1.cbn.com/biblestudy/theology-q%26a-holy-spirit

Lesson 2
The Message of the Church

Knowing the mission of the church depends on how we define our message. Our message is simple; Jesus and the kingdom. Yet, despite its simplicity, many in the church world get it wrong. If you are not sure, ask 10 Christian friends to give a definition of the Gospel. There may be common themes, but as you find out, there is even greater disparity on what exactly is the 'gospel message.' So, what is our message?

Those embracing the present kingdom are regularly blamed for 'disregarding the cross.' This may have happened. Because of our excitement about the revelation of the kingdom of God, other aspects, like the cross, might have gotten lost for a season. Usually when a truth is restored there is a swing too far and over time it balances out. Should we put the kingdom on the shelf for a while and return to the cross? If we do, then an even greater distortion would happen, as the 'purpose of the cross' would be lost. The kingdom and the cross are aspects of one message, one gospel. With the renewed interest in the *Christus Victor* view of the atonement, many are 'returning to the cross' without abandoning the revelation of the kingdom.

> *For God so loved the world that he gave his only Son, that whoever believes in him should not perish but have eternal life.* (John 3:16)

In this verse we have the gospel from God's side and our perspective. God was moved by love. The love of God would not allow humanity to be trapped in realms of darkness, ruled by sin and death. The love of God was the motivation for giving His Son. Our responsibility and response to God's demonstration of Divine love is simple; believe.

Jesus' most difficult assignment was not healing the sick or delivering those afflicted by evil powers, it was simply, "Believe that the Father sent Me".

> *For God did not send his Son into the world to condemn the world, but in order that the world might be saved through Him.* (John 3:17)

When Jesus came into the world in His incarnation, it was not to condemn the world, but to save it. Nothing has changed. God's desire is saving the world, not destroying it through judgment. Any end-time view, which sees total destruction as God's purpose, misses this vital point.

> *Because, if you confess with your mouth that Jesus is Lord and believe in your heart that God raised him from the dead, you will be saved.* (Romans 10:9)

Apostle Paul adds that confession (agreement) that Jesus is God's Messiah and belief in His resurrection is needed. In presenting the gospel message, the resurrection of Jesus is a required element. In other places, 'repentance' is mentioned, but not here. Can a person be saved without repenting?

> *Then they said to him, "What must we do, to be doing the works of God?" Jesus answered them, "This is the work of God, that you believe in Him whom He has sent".* (John 6:28-29)

Again, the central point is simply, 'believe.' What are we to believe; that Jesus is the One (the prophesied Messiah) sent from God.

> *To Him all the prophets bear witness that everyone who believes in Him receives forgiveness of sins through His name.* (Acts 10:43)

We now have a verse, which mentions 'forgiveness of sins.' Notice the order, first we believe (and according to the other passages we are saved) then we receive forgiveness of sin. What is the modern Evangelical order? Repent of your sins, then ask Jesus into your heart and then you will be saved.

> *But God shows his love for us in that while we were still sinners, Christ died for us.*
> (Romans 5:8)

God sent His Son to redeem the world. But how will that be accomplished? Jesus came and 'died for us.' The cross with its shame and violence is the path Jesus took, to deliver us out of our realms of darkness with its shame and violence. The messenger of peace endured violence, so we can live in the covenant of peace (Is. 54:10). Jesus experienced death, so we can experience life.

> *Now after John was arrested, Jesus came into Galilee, proclaiming the gospel of God, and saying, "The time is fulfilled, and the kingdom of God is at hand repent and believe in the gospel."* (Mark 1:14-15)

At the start of His ministry, Jesus explains the gospel in kingdom terms. He tells us the gospel (good news) is the arrival of the kingdom. I assume the time Jesus spoke of refers to the book of Daniel, where it was revealed that in 490 years the events of the coming Messiah would unfold. The proclamation of the gospel is amazingly straightforward; Jesus came and established God's kingdom on earth. That is the good news we share. Why is that good news? In the kingdom we are forgiven of sin, we receive the Spirit, we are united in fellowship with the Father, we receive the blessings of Abraham, we enter the new covenant and we have eternal life. And this is just the beginning, there is a lot more. When we are born into the kingdom of God we have the whole package which is called salvation.

> *After John was arrested, Jesus went to Galilee preaching the Message of God: "Time's up! God's kingdom is here. Change your life and believe the Message."* (The Message Bible: Mark 1:14-15)

> *But he said to them, "I must preach the good news of the kingdom of God to the other towns as well; for I was sent for this purpose."* (Luke 4:43)

There should be little doubt that the message of Jesus was that the kingdom of God was at hand, at the time when He was preaching it! He was not referring to events several thousand years in the future. Our message is the same, believe that Jesus is God's Messiah and enter the kingdom.

Gospel Definitions

The following definitions and many more have been compiled by Trevor Wax and can be found at his website.[3]

William Tyndale

"Evangelion (that we call the gospel) is a Greek word and signifieth good, merry, glad and joyful tidings, that maketh a man's heart glad and maketh him sing, dance, and leap for joy… [This gospel is] all of Christ the right David, how that he hath fought with sin, with death, and the devil, and overcome them: whereby all men that were in bondage to sin, wounded with death, overcome of the devil are without their own merits or deserving's loosed, justified, restored to life and saved, brought to liberty and reconciled unto the favor of God and set at one with him again: which tidings as many as believe laud, praise and thank God, are glad, sing and dance for joy."[4]

Tyndale's opening sentence is great. Yes, the gospel should make us 'leap for joy.' He also covers the important aspects of David and the kingdom connection, the defeat of death, sin and the satan. He includes our being reconciled with God and restored to life. I like Tyndale's definition.

Mike Wittmer

"Hear the Christian gospel: We are all rebellious traitors against God and his kingdom, and for that we are dying now and are destined to suffer forever in the ultimate despair of hell. We are actually God's enemies (not merely in our imagination), and we deserve whatever torment we have coming. Worse, we are entirely unable to lay down our weapons and change sides, for as the apostle Paul reminds us, we are "dead in our transgressions and sins... by nature deserving of wrath... without hope and without God in the world" (Eph. 2:1-12). We are unwilling to change, and unable to change our hearts and minds so we would be willing."[5]

In fairness to Wittmer, he wrote four paragraphs, yet, for brevity and to see a different beginning point, I include only his opening words. Is this how the presentation of the gospel should begin? I know this is exactly the way many Evangelicals would begin their presentation; by explaining how bad and sinful we are and why God should, rightfully, throw us all into hell. I am thankful many are re-thinking the starting point of our gospel message.

Andy Crouch

"The gospel is the proclamation of Jesus, in [two] senses. It is the proclamation announced by Jesus – the arrival of God's realm of possibility (his "kingdom") in the midst of human structures of possibility. But it is also the proclamation about Jesus – the good news that in dying and rising, Jesus has made the kingdom he proclaimed available to us."

Crouch catches the essence of the gospel, when he defines the kingdom as "God's realm of possibility". I like that!

Tim Keller

The 'gospel' is the good news that through Christ the power of God's kingdom has entered history to renew the whole world. When we believe and rely on Jesus' work and record (rather than ours) for our relationship to God, that kingdom power comes upon us and begins to work through us."

Keller accentuates the point of God's kingdom entering history.

C.H. Dodd

"The Gospel" Summarized in 6 Parts

1. The Age of Fulfillment has dawned, the "latter days" fo retold by the prophets (Acts 3:18-26).

2. This has taken place through the birth, life, ministry, de ath and resurrection of Jesus Christ (Acts 2:22-31).

3. By virtue of the resurrection, Jesus has been exalted at t he right hand of God as Messianic head of the new Israel (Acts 2:32-36).

4. The Holy Spirit in the church is the sign of Christ's pre sent power and glory (Acts 10:44-48).

5. The Messianic Age will reach its consummation in the r eturn of Christ (Acts 3:20-21).

6. An appeal is made for repentance with the offer of forgi veness, the Holy Spirit, and salvation (Acts 2:37-41)."

I find Dodd's definition one of the most complete and it addresses many important points to the understanding the gospel we preach.

Scot McKnight

"The gospel is the work of God to restore humans to union with God and communion with others, in the context of a community, for the good of others and the world."

This definition takes us beyond 'individual salvation' to the context of community to reach the world.

Ed Stetzer

"The gospel is the good news that God, who is more holy than we can imagine, looked upon with compassion, people, who are more sinful than we would possibly admit, and sent Jesus into history to establish his Kingdom and reconcile people and the world to himself. Jesus, who love is more extravagant than we can measure, came to sacrificially die for us so that, by his death and resurrection, we might gain through His grace what the Bible defines as new and eternal life."

N.T. Wright

"The gospel is the royal announcement that the crucified and risen Jesus, who died for our sins and rose again according to the Scriptures, has been enthroned as the true Lord of the world. When this gospel is preached, God calls people to salvation, out of sheer grace, leading them to repentance and faith in Jesus Christ as the risen Lord."

I find Wright's view that the gospel is a 'royal announcement' refreshing, because as we preach 'this gospel', then by God's grace people are saved. Our task is to make the announcement.

Robert A. Guelich

"The answer to our dilemma of how the gospel of the Kingdom and the gospel of the cross relate is that the gospel of the cross is integral to the gospel of the Kingdom if we understand both to mean expression of the same "gospel" then is the message that God acted in and through Jesus Messiah, God's anointed one, to effect God's promise of shalom, salvation, God's reign."[6]

Here is a definition provided by a Christian organization.

IVP Dictionary of the New Testament

"GOSPEL (Good News) – See "Kingdom of God"

Thank you, InterVarsity Press!

If a greater percentage of churches would think 'kingdom' when they hear the word 'gospel', the church would be much further along in advancing the kingdom and discipling the nations.

Do we proclaim the kingdom or individual salvation?

Trever Wax says: "It seems that two opposing camps are forming. The first camp believes we have truncated the gospel by only focusing on individual salvation at the expense of the cosmic dimension of Jesus' lordship. Furthermore, by neglecting the biblical teaching about the coming Kingdom of God, some worry that we have embraced a gospel that is so heaven-centered as to render it ineffective to speak to earthly realities."

Trever Wax continues about these two opposing views of the gospel: "It is frustrating to me that the two camps expect us to choose between these two options as if they were mutually exclusive. If the gospel is the announcement of Jesus Christ – specifically his death and resurrection and exaltation as Lord of the world – then we have a message that is both personal and cosmic. It is a message about the coming of God's kingdom, yes. And the king of that kingdom has given his life for its subjects (atonement)."[7]

When the church begins to grasp a larger and more biblical announcement of the Gospel, we will begin to see that there is no separation in preaching the cross and preaching the kingdom. The cross and resurrection are the door into the kingdom.

Discussion and Questions

1. Do you see aspects of William Tyndale's definition being '*Christus Victor*', concerning his understanding of the gospel?

2. What has been your presentation of the gospel in the past and will it change in the future?

3. Which definition do you like best?

4. Do we have two gospels - one of salvation and one of the kingdom?

5. What 'atonement doctrine' best brings out individual salvation and the world changing power of the kingdom?

6. What should a person 'know' to be saved? What should they 'experience' to be saved?

Footnotes

[3] Gospel Definitions: www.trevinwax.com

[4] William Tyndale, *A Pathway into the Holy Scripture*, 1531

[5] Michael Wittmer, *Christ Alone: An Evangelical Response to Rob Bell's Love Wins* (148-150)

[6] What is the Gospel? Inaugural Address, Fuller Theological Seminary, May 9

[7]

https://blogs.thegospelcoalition.org/trevinwax/2008/06/17/the-gospel-of-god-personal-atonement-or-christs-kingdom/

Lesson 3
The Church and the Old Testament Scripture

For several decades the early church relied solely on the Old Testament for its inspired Scripture. The bulk of the New Testament was written between 50-65 A.D. So, for the first several decades, the early church had one Bible; the Old Testament. How did they understand it? Was it different from how we read it today? Unfortunately, we have only portions of New Testament commentary on the ancient Scriptures, yet, they provide an open door as to how they should be read.

If we are reading Israel's history, the psalms or proverbs, everything seems straightforward. There is a common literary sense of reading wisdom literature, poetry or history that is familiar. The problem comes when we get to the prophets. Will King David really rebuild his tent / tabernacle? Will the kingdom of Israel continue without end? Will a literal river flow out of a rebuilt temple? Will animal sacrifices continue in the age of the kingdom? It can be confusing. Most Evangelicals have grown up with the rule of a literal interpretation of Scripture. Although this is a good place to begin, it does not always work, especially in the Old Testament.

When the old prophets spoke, we cannot be sure of how much revelation they had concerning the words they spoke. Were they speaking of soon coming events within their time or culture, or did they understand their words would later be read as Messianic? When the prophets speak of the restoration of Israel and about natural blessings, we are seeing a glorious and blessed church, yet, for the prophet, it would have been difficult to have that kind of understanding. We do know that a few possessed greater understanding. Apostle Peter tells us that David *"spoke about the resurrection of the Christ"* (Acts 2:31).

I'm suggesting we expand our hermeneutical tools to include aspects of a Christocentric approach. Another term in the academic world is, *Theological Interpretation of Scripture*. These ways of interpreting Scripture are scholarly and academic studies in hermeneutics which are beyond the scope or purpose of these lessons. However, since they are helpful in pursuing a kingdom / new covenant understanding, I will simplify few of their basic principles.

1. Jesus is the purest, the most complete, and the highest revelation of who God is.

2. The God of the Old Testament must be see through the lens of Jesus, hence, Christocentric.

3. Jesus is the final expression of God and therefore He is the authoritative standard to interpret all Scripture, including the Old Testament.

4. To understand the whole of Scripture it is imperative we have a 'New Covenant' revelation. Therefore, we read from a "Theological Interpretation' based on the new covenant.

It will be difficult to arrive at a Christocentric hermeneutic, unless we first embrace the principles of a 'Kingdom / New Covenant' perspective.

New Testament Scriptures Affirming the Centrality of Christ

He is the image of the invisible God, the firstborn of all creation. For by him all things were created, in heaven and on earth, visible and invisible, whether thrones or dominions or rulers or authorities—all things were created through him and for him. And he is before all things, and in him all things hold together. And he is the head of the body, the church. He is the beginning, the firstborn from the dead, that in everything he might be preeminent. For in him all the fullness of God was pleased to dwell, and through him to reconcile to himself all things, whether on earth or in heaven, making peace by the blood of his cross. (Colossians 1:15-20)

In this amazing passage, Apostle Paul places Jesus, the Messiah, in the position of fulfilling the exact things ascribed to the Father. This is like other New Testament authors, who placed Jesus as the One, who was in the beginning with the Father. The key part is where Paul states *"In him all the fullness of God was pleased to dwell."*

That their hearts may be encouraged, being knit together in love, to reach all the riches of full assurance of understanding and the knowledge of God's mystery, which is Christ, in whom are hidden all the treasures of wisdom and knowledge. (Colossians 2:2-3)

I am the way, and the truth, and the life. (John 14:6)

Jesus did not say He was 'one truth among many,' but that He was *the* truth, the final truth. He is the only way to the Father and He is the only expression of the Father's life.

All things have been handed over to me by my Father, and no one knows the Son except the Father, and no one knows the Father except the Son and anyone to whom the Son chooses to reveal Him. (Matthew 11:27)

What needs to be recognized, is that Jesus is a higher authority than Moses or the Prophets, in understanding the Father. We do not discount the revelation of these previous leaders, but we submit their writings to be viewed from the perspective of Jesus.

Pastor and theologian Greg Boyd states, "These earliest disciples assumed, as did the church tradition that followed them, that Jesus was "the goal and fulfillment of the whole

Old Testament" and therefore, "the interpretive key to the Bible."[8]

What was the foundation behind the early church's 'Christocentric' hermeneutic? It was a Holy Spirit inspired theology that Jesus was the Messiah and therefore He taught that the Old Testament spoke of Him. First, they adopted a theology of Jesus, then, built their hermeneutic upon their theology.

Boyd goes further and expands upon what is was the Apostles considered before interpreting the Old Testament.

"The authors of the NT were not interested in discerning the original meaning of passages to place alongside of the revelation of God in Christ; they were rather intent on discerning the meaning passages had when read in the light of Christ. This "new" and "creative" approach was adopted by NT authors because in the words of Moule, "Christ was found to be more authoritative than scripture…in the sense of fulfilling and transcending it, not abolishing it."[9]

Boyd throws down the gauntlet to the modern church, which has become addicted to a 'literal interpretation' of Scripture and our search for the authors' original meanings. Of course, both can be useful for a correct understanding, but can also, if not properly used, be a strait jacket. I affirm Boyd's conclusions and suggest we go back to the drawing boards and rebuilt our methods of Scriptural interpretation upon these principles.

Jesus knew the importance of the Old Testament, because it contained revelation about Him.

> *And beginning with Moses and all the Prophets, He interpreted to them in all the Scriptures the things concerning Himself.* (Luke 24:27)

Here are a few examples of Apostolic interpretation of Scripture.

> *"Sing, O barren one, who did not bear; break forth into singing and cry aloud, you who*

have not been in labor! For the children of the desolate one will be more than the children of her who is married," says the Lord. "Enlarge the place of your tent, and let the curtains of your habitations be stretched out; do not hold back; lengthen your cords and strengthen your stakes. For you will spread abroad to the right and to the left, and your offspring will possess the nations and will people the desolate cities". (Isaiah 54:1-3)

Our first step is to ask who are the *"Children of the desolate one"* and who are the *"Children of her who is married."* Israel was the only nation who was married to the one true God. Those referred to as *'desolate'* are Gentiles. What is the prophecy concerning these two groups? A major change will take place where the Gentiles will outnumber the children of Israel in the family of God.

Apostle Paul uses these words of Isaiah in teaching about the two covenants.

> For it is written that Abraham had two sons, one by a slave woman and one by a free woman. But the son of the slave was born according to the flesh, while the son of the free woman was born through promise. Now this may be interpreted allegorically: these women are two covenants. One is from Mount Sinai, bearing children for slavery; she is Hagar. Now Hagar is Mount Sinai in Arabia; she corresponds to the present Jerusalem, for she is in slavery with her children. But the Jerusalem above is free, and she is our mother. For it is written,
>
> *"Rejoice, O barren one who does not bear; break forth and cry aloud, you who are not in labor!*

> *For the children of the desolate one will be more than those of the one who has a husband.* " (Galatians 4:22-27)

Paul compares the two women in Abraham's life, who bore him children. One woman was a slave and her son was not the child of promise. The other woman was free, and the son born was the one promised by God. Paul uses a rather unorthodox hermeneutic. He says these two women are 'covenants' and then says they are 'mountains' which represent the two covenants. Then he quotes Isaiah about the two women, one who is desolate and the other married.

The first covenant is a symbol of the physical Jerusalem at the time of Paul. This is the old covenant with its Temple worship and Mosaic Law. The second covenant was established by Christ and was the new covenant prophesied by Jeremiah. The new covenant is based upon the son of promise. It is the church. It is the new Jerusalem. The church will far exceed the number of a single nation. The church will expand to all nations and peoples.

What is important in this example is how that Paul went back and re-read Isaiah, considering Christ and the new covenant. This shows he used the theology of his present understanding, to correctly interpret an Old Testament passage. This is an example of a Christo-Centric interpretation.

> *In that day I will raise up the booth of David that is fallen and repair its breaches, and raise up its ruins and rebuild it as in the days of old.* (Amos 9:11)

Amos speaks of a day when Israel will be in their land and will enjoy great blessings. He says in this time of restoration, that David's 'booth' or tent / tabernacle will be rebuilt. This sounds rather easy to interpret. Someday in the future, Israel will return to their land, rebuilt David's tabernacle and live in prosperity. For Dispensationalists, this is exactly the type of passages they point to, for the return of

Israel in 1948. Yet, if we follow this line of reasoning, that, the 'literal reading' is the exclusive hermeneutical method, then, we would have missed the central point of Amos's prophecy. How do we know this? Because Apostle James in Acts 15 provides the 'apostolic' or correct theological interpretation.

> But some men came down from Judea and were teaching the brothers, "Unless you are circumcised according to the custom of Moses, you cannot be saved". And after Paul and Barnabas had no small dissension and debate with them, Paul and Barnabas and some of the others were appointed to go up to Jerusalem to the apostles and the elders about this question. (Acts 15:1-2)

When Gentiles began to embrace Jesus, it brought about a key question concerning the relationship between the old and the new covenant. The current thinking of the day was, "We are Jews and therefore we keep the Mosaic Law", but what about the Gentiles?" When a dispute broke out an Apostolic council was scheduled.

> But some believers who belonged to the party of the Pharisees rose up and said, "It is necessary to circumcise them and to order them to keep the law of Moses." (Acts 15:5)

Apostle Peter speaks of the miracle of the Gentiles conversion and challenges the leaders,

> "And after there had been much debate, Peter stood up and said to them, "Brothers, you know that in the early days God made a choice among you, that by my mouth the Gentiles should hear the word of the gospel and believe. And God, who knows the heart, bore witness to them, by giving them the Holy Spirit just as he did to us, and he made no

distinction between us and them, having cleansed their hearts by faith. Now, therefore, why are you putting God to the test by placing a yoke on the neck of the disciples that neither our fathers nor we have been able to bear? But we believe that we will be saved through the grace of the Lord Jesus, just as they will" (Acts 15:7-11).

I find it interesting that Peter referred to the Mosaic law as a yoke, or we can say, a heavy burden. Then, Barnabas and Paul tell their experience with the Gentiles. Finally, Apostle James, the presiding Elder in the Jerusalem church, made the conclusion.

How does James present his case and what authority does he ascribe to? James accepts that God is bringing Gentiles to faith. The Holy Spirit has made that clear. Then, he goes to the only written authority they have, the Old Testament Scripture.

And with this the words of the prophets agree, just as it is written,

" 'After this I will return, and I will rebuild the tent of David that has fallen; I will rebuild its ruins, and I will restore it, that the remnant of mankind may seek the Lord, and all the Gentiles who are called by my name, says the Lord, who makes these things known from of old.' (Acts 15:15-17)

What just happened? James uses a new covenant-Christo-centric hermeneutic, to understand Amos. He declares that the fulfillment of David rebuilding his tabernacle says nothing about a physical structure or ethnic Israel being prosperous in their land, but declares the fulfillment of Amos is the inclusion of Gentiles into the church of Jesus.

Their conclusion is that the Law of Moses is not binding for salvation on the Gentiles. Yet, because of the Jewish culture they lived in, the Apostles and Elders gave them several things to avoid, "*abstain from the things polluted by idols, and from sexual immorality, and from what has been strangled, and from blood*" (Acts 15:20).

For the church to fully grasp the extent of the kingdom of God, we cannot exclude the many Old Testament prophetic passages. In them we find a fuller description of the kingdom age in which we are living.

Discussion and Questions

1. Even though Gentiles were '*free from the Law*" in Acts 15, to what extent do you think the believing Jews followed the rules of 'Temple worship', before the revelation that not only Gentiles, but even Jews were free from the Law of Moses?

2. What can we learn about the present and advancing kingdom of God on earth from the Old Testament Prophets? Give examples.

3. Discuss some basics of 'New Covenant Theology' that would be essential to correctly interpret the Old Testament?

4. What will be the role of the Holy Spirt in applying a Christo-centric hermeneutic?

Footnotes
[8] Greg Boyd, *Crucifixion of the Warrior God*, Fortress Press, Minneapolis, page 95

[9] Greg Boyd, *Crucifixion of the Warrior God*, Fortress Press, Minneapolis, page 98

Lesson 4
The Roots of the Church - Part 1

The Day of Pentecost was the first day of the new covenant church. From that day forward, everything was different. Nevertheless, we must recognize that the church was not born into a vacuum. The roots of the church are in the prophetic words of the Prophets and in the covenants made with Abraham and David.

Dispensationalists claim the church was not seen or foretold in the Old Testament. They see the church as an entirely new thing God birthed, after Israel rejected Jesus as their Messiah. This is not true! The testimony of the New Testament Apostles claims the church is fulfilling what the Prophets spoke of. The church's roots are found throughout the prophetic pages of the Old Testament.

> *I am speaking the truth in Christ—I am not lying; my conscience bears me witness in the Holy Spirit— that I have great sorrow and unceasing anguish in my heart. For I could wish that I myself were accursed and cut off from Christ for the sake of my brothers my kinsmen according to the flesh. They are Israelites, and to them belong the adoption, the glory, the covenants, the giving of the law, the worship, and the promises. To them belong the patriarchs, and from their race, according to the flesh, is the Christ, who is God over all, blessed forever. Amen.* (Romans 9:1-5)

Apostle Paul did not believe Israel could maintain any relationship with their God apart from their Messiah. This brought him great sorrow. He then reminds his readers (and us today), that Israel was vital to God's plan of renewing the world through Christ. To them (not the gentiles), belonged "*the adoption, the glory, the covenants, the giving of the law, the worship, and the promises.*" Without Israel, there would be no savior for the world. It was through this people that Jesus was born in the flesh.

Who Are the offspring of Abraham?

> *But it is not as though the word of God has failed. For not all who are descended from Israel belong to Israel, and not all are children of Abraham because they are his offspring, but "Through Isaac shall your offspring be named." This means that it is not the children of the flesh who are the children of God, but the children of the promise are counted as offspring.* (Romans 9:6-8)

Israel is to be honored for their history. But this honor and appreciation does not give them freedom to reject God's Christ. Claiming to be the offspring of Abraham, but rejecting the promise, separated them from God.

A Remnant

> *And Isaiah cries out concerning Israel: "Though the number of the sons of Israel be as the sand of the sea, only a remnant of them will be saved".* (Romans 9:27)

This verse comes from a longer passage in Isaiah.

> *In that day the remnant of Israel and the survivors of the house of Jacob will no more lean on him who struck them, but will lean on the Lord, the Holy One of Israel, in truth.*

A remnant will return, the remnant of Jacob, to the mighty God. For though your people Israel be as the sand of the sea, only a remnant of them will return. Destruction is decreed, overflowing with righteousness. For the Lord God of hosts will make a full end, as decreed, in the midst of all the earth. (Isaiah 10:20-23)

Apostle Paul is building his argument line upon line. First, we must honor Israel for its past. Second, Israel cannot get a free pass, because they claim Abraham as their father. Third, we cannot then conclude that Israel has been rejected. Why? Because by God's grace there is a minority within Israel who accepted their Messiah.

Brothers my heart's desire and prayer to God for them is that they may be saved. For I bear them witness that they have a zeal for God, but not according to knowledge. For, being ignorant of the righteousness of God, and seeking to establish their own, they did not submit to God's righteousness. For Christ is the end of the law for righteousness to everyone who believes. (Romans 10:1-4)

Israel had a zeal for God, but their zeal was in the wrong belief system. Their entire religious life was wrapped up in the Torah, the books of Moses. While rejecting Jesus as the Christ, they maintained their righteousness, based upon the Law of Moses. Big mistake! The people of Israel received more knowledge of God than any other people, yet, they were *"ignorant of the righteousness of God"*. The righteousness of God was now fully revealed in Jesus. Jesus brought about the end of the law.

I ask, then, has God rejected his people? By no means! For I myself am an Israelite, a descendant of Abraham, a member of the tribe of Benjamin. God has not rejected his people whom he foreknew. Do you not know what the Scripture says of Elijah, how he appeals to God against Israel? "Lord, they have killed your prophets, they have demolished your altars, and I alone am left, and they seek my life." But what is God's reply to him? "I have kept for myself seven thousand men who have not bowed the knee to Baal." So too at the present time there is a remnant, chosen by grace. But if it is by grace, it is no longer on the basis of works; otherwise grace would no longer be grace. (Romans 11:1-7)

What then? Israel failed to obtain what it was seeking. The elect obtained it, but the rest were hardened.

Those who claim that kingdom / new covenant people believe in a 'Replacement Theology', must follow Paul's argument more closely. God has not rejected His people? Why? Because there is a remnant from Israel, embracing Jesus as the Christ. They now are God's Israel. They are the heirs of the covenants and promises found in the Old Testament. They are the new eschatological Israel.

I love the example Sam Storms uses to define the connection between Israel and the church.

"And when I look at the relationship between Israel and the Church, I see something similar to the relationship between the caterpillar and the butterfly. The butterfly doesn't replace the caterpillar. The butterfly IS the caterpillar, in a more developed and consummate form. The butterfly is what God intended the caterpillar to become. Likewise, the church doesn't replace Israel. The church IS Israel, as God always intended it to be."[10]

What happened to the majority of Israel, who did not believe? Those who insisted the 'caterpillar' stage was all they needed? They came under the pronouncement of judgment.

Even John the Baptist knew this would happen.

> *But when he saw many of the Pharisees and Sadducees coming to his baptism, he said to them, "You brood of vipers! Who warned you to flee from the wrath to come? Bear fruit in keeping with repentance. And do not presume to say to yourselves, 'We have Abraham as our father,' for I tell you, God is able from these stones to raise up children for Abraham. Even now the axe is laid to the root of the trees. Every tree therefore that does not bear good fruit is cut down and thrown into the fire.* (Matthew 3:7-10)

The religious leaders of Israel were warned about a coming judgement. Two key elements are found in this early passage in the Gospels.

> 1. Attempting to connect with Abraham will not work.

> 2. God is looking for fruit.

John the Baptist said that the axe is already laid to the root. This was spoken about 30 A.D. The tree fell one generation later. The judgment was the destruction of the Temple and the city of Jerusalem. Both were destroyed under the Roman General Titus and his armies, in the fall of 70 A.D.

Jesus spoke this same theme of judgment and lack of fruit. After telling the story about the tenants of the vineyard, He made the following solemn statement.

> *Therefore I tell you, the kingdom of God will be taken away from you and given to a people producing its fruits.* (Matthew 21:43)

43

With this background Apostle Paul tells how Gentiles can be included in the new Israel of God - the believing remnant.

> *Now I am speaking to you Gentiles. Inasmuch then as I am an apostle to the Gentiles, I magnify my ministry in order somehow to make my fellow Jews jealous, and thus save some of them.* (Romans 11:13-14)

Paul magnifies his ministry to the Gentiles, to bring as many Jews back into the faith, as possible.

Grafted In

> *But if some of the branches were broken off, and you, although a wild olive shoot, were grafted in among the others and now share in the nourishing root of the olive tree.* (Romans 11:17)

Gentiles are included in God's great plan. Through Jesus the Messiah, all peoples of all nations can join in and experience the blessings of Israel - the new Israel of God. The first years of the church was entirely made up of this remnant - the Jews who accepted Jesus. It is this Israel that we are grafted into; not unbelieving Israel. This is a key to understanding how the church is built upon the roots, the rich roots of the covenants and promises found in the Old Testament.

The promises made by the Prophets are not for a political nation. They are for true Israel, the remnant, which Apostle Paul belonged to and which believing Gentiles are grafted into. Together, Jew and Gentile are the "*one new man*" (Eph. 2:15).

In the next lesson we turn to the Old Testament and examine a few of The Prophetic Roots of the Church.

Discussion and Questions

1. In Roman 11:1 Paul asks, *"Has God rejected His people"*? The answer is: "No!" Then, in verse 15 he says, *"Their rejection"* will bring about the salvation of the world. What does this mean? Who was not rejected in verse one and who is rejected in verse 15?

2. How do we honor Israel for being the people through whom God brought the promises, the covenants and finally the Messiah? Should the present nation called Israel be honored for what God gave a people over 2,000 years ago?

3. Have you attempted to explain to another Christian how the church is not a type or symbol of Israel, but the church is Israel (although a newly reformed Israel centered around Jesus and His new covenant)? What was the result? How can this concept be explained better to those still embracing dispensationalism?

4. Since new covenant believers are grafted into the rich roots of biblical Israel, should this challenge us to study the Old Testament more?

Footnotes
[10] http://www.samstorms.com/enjoying-god-blog/post/replacement-theology-or-inclusion-theology

Lesson 5
The Roots of the Church -
Part Two

We are grafted into the roots of Israel. Because of Jesus, we have legal access to all the prophetic words spoken over Israel. Volumes can (and should) be written about the prophetic word for the new covenant church. The book of Psalms includes numerous passages concerning the coming reign of a David, because he was a type of the Messiah. All through the Prophets, we have passage after passage of prophetic words, which are our inheritance.

To understand these prophetic words in relationship to the new covenant church, a hermeneutic using a 'Theological Interpretation' is needed. This includes a Christocentric view of the Old Testament. What does this mean? It means we do not interpret the Old Testament apart from the New Testament. The New Testament is the commentary on the Old. The revelation of Jesus and the Apostles are the higher and true understanding of what the Prophets spoke. This means the understanding of the Jesus and the Apostles may be different from the authors original intention, yet is the true revelation.

Throughout the Old Testament and especially in the Prophets there are passages which shed light on the new covenant church. Yet, for space and time, our lesson will review only the book of Isaiah. He was truly a kingdom / new covenant prophet.

For to us a child is born, to us a son is given; and the government shall be upon his shoulder, and his name shall be called Wonderful Counselor, Mighty God, Everlasting Father, Prince of Peace. Of the increase of his government and of peace there will be no end, on the throne of David and over his kingdom, to establish it and to uphold it with justice and with righteousness from this time forth and forevermore. The zeal of the Lord of hosts will do this. (Isaiah 9:6-7)

Dispensationalists take an interesting path in interpreting this passage. Scholars across various theological persuasions agree that this is clearly a Messianic passage. Yet, leave it to dispensationalists to take the simple and complicate it. Here is their version. God gives Jesus in the incarnation and then after several thousand years He is given the kingdom. Between the words "given" and "government" there is a huge gap of time. According to this theory, the kingdom is waiting for the Second Coming and only then will the kingdom be established in the earth.

There is no hint, no textual nor historical reason, to divide the birth of Jesus from His bringing in of the kingdom of God. How long will this kingdom - the fulfillment of the Davidic covenant - last? It has no end.

In days to come Jacob shall take root, Israel shall blossom and put forth shoots and fill the whole world with fruit. (Isaiah 27:6)

This is one of my favorite verses from Isaiah. Yet, I am confounded by how many misses what should be obvious. This is not about modern Israel filling the world with avocados and mangoes. Much of Scripture is about God desiring His people to be fruitful.

When Jesus came, He found Israel as a fruitless nation and this was a key reason they lost the kingdom (Matthew 21:43). The church is called to be a fruitful nation that fills the world with the goodness of God.

> *Behold my servant, whom I uphold, my chosen, in whom my soul delights; I have put my Spirit upon him; He will bring forth justice to the nations. He will not cry aloud or lift up His voice, or make it heard in the street; a bruised reed He will not break, and a faintly burning wick He will not quench; He will faithfully bring forth justice He will not grow faint or be discouraged till he has established justice in the earth; and the coastlands wait for His law.* (Isaiah 42:1-4)

The passages about the "servant" are widely accepted by biblical scholars as Messianic. The difference is in the timing of the work of the Messiah in bringing *"justice to the nations."* Whenever Old Testament passages speak of the Messiah and His work among the nations, dispensationalists separate His 'kingdom' activity from His saving work. They teach His first coming did not establish the kingdom of God but was postponed until He returns a second time.

There is nothing in the words of Isaiah that would cause us to separate His 'receiving the Spirit' from His work of bringing justice to the nations. One leads to the other. We make a mistake, when we lose sight of the mission of the church, which carries on the ministry of Jesus in the earth. With King Jesus guiding us, the church will bring justice to the nations.

The last line is interesting in that it speaks of the law of the Messiah. The question we need to ask, is "What law?" It is not the 'Law of Moses" that will transform the nations; it is the Law of Christ. His Law - that is what we need.

He says:

> *"It is too light a thing that you should be my servant to raise up the tribes of Jacob and to bring back the preserved of Israel; I will make you as a light for the nations, that my salvation may reach to the end of the earth."*
> (Isaiah 49:6)

Is this a restoration passage for the nation of Israel? Without applying basic principles of new covenant theology, it would be easy to think that. We cannot fully interpret these Old Testament prophetic verses separate from the coming of Jesus and the new covenant. It is passages like this and many others that become the 'roots' of the church.

Who are these people that bring salvation to the nations? It is the church. This is our promise. This is part of being grafted into the rich roots of Israel.

Isaiah 54:1, 10, 13

This passage was covered in chapter three and we remember that when Isaiah predicted *"For the children of the desolate one will be more than the children of her who is married"* it means Gentiles will outnumber the children of Israel. It has new covenant applications.

Verse 10

> *For the mountains may depart and the hills be removed, but My steadfast love shall not depart from you, and my covenant of peace shall not be removed,"* says the Lord, who has compassion on you.

Is the 'covenant of peace' a reference to the old covenant of Moses? I would say: "No!" Or, is it an Old Testament expression of what Jeremiah will rename later and call the 'new covenant'?

Verse 13

All your children shall be taught by the Lord,
and great shall be the peace of your children.

The reason our children will be taught of the Lord is because all members of the body of Christ have the Holy Spirit within them. This is new covenant truth. When Jeremiah wrote a few hundred years later he said something very similar.

> *"For this is the covenant that I will make with the house of Israel after those days, declares the Lord: I will put my law within them, and I will write it on their hearts. And I will be their God, and they shall be my people. And no longer shall each one teach his neighbor and each his brother, saying, 'Know the Lord,' for they shall all know me, from the least of them to the greatest, declares the Lord. For I will forgive their iniquity, and I will remember their sin no more."* (Jeremiah 31:33-34)

Within the context of the new covenant is a 'covenant of peace.' There is a great deal of Scriptural support that 'peace' is one of the primary attributes of God and should be of the church also.

Isaiah 9:6 Jesus is the "prince of peace."

Ephesians 2:13 Apostle Paul says, *"He is our peace"*, and that Jesus *"preached peace"*.

Matthew 5:9 *"Blessed are the peacemakers, for they shall be called sons of God"*.

Romans 14:17 *"For the kingdom of God is not a matter of eating and drinking but of righteousness and peace and joy in the Holy Spirit"*.

II Corinthians 13:11 *"Finally, brothers, rejoice. Aim for restoration, comfort one another, agree with one another, live in peace; and the God of love and peace will be with you."*

The gospel is the message and the lifestyle of peace. Have we forgotten that?

> *Come, everyone who thirsts, come to the waters; and he who has no money, come, buy and eat! Come, buy wine and milk without money and without price. Why do you spend your money for that which is not bread, and your labor for that which does not satisfy? Listen diligently to me, and eat what is good, and delight yourselves in rich food. Incline your ear, and come to me; hear, that your soul may live; and I will make with you an everlasting covenant, my steadfast, sure love for David.* (Isaiah 55:1-3)

Isaiah begins with an unusual offer. He invites people to buy wine and milk for free. He asks why they buy bread that does not satisfy. The key to understanding this passage is in its connection it to the new covenant, where Jesus is our daily bread. The 'everlasting covenant' is the new covenant. We know this, because the only covenant that fulfills the Davidic covenant is the new covenant.

> *And a Redeemer will come to Zion, to those in Jacob who turn from transgression,"* declares the Lord.
>
> *"And as for me, this is my covenant with them,"* says the Lord: *"My Spirit that is upon you, and my words that I have put in your mouth, shall not depart out of your mouth, or out of the mouth of your offspring, or out of the mouth of your children's offspring,"* says the Lord, *"from this time forth and forevermore."* (Isaiah 59:20-21)

Isaiah starts with identifying the people he speaks about. The Redeemer is the Messiah. It is Jesus. The people of the covenant will be those from old covenant Israel who turn or repent. This is exactly what Jesus announced.

> *"Repent, for the kingdom of heaven is at hand"* (Matthew 4:17).

What is a key element in this new covenant? It is the Holy Spirit. This promise is a generational promise. It goes on and on for *"forevermore."*

> *Arise, shine, for your light has come, and the glory of the Lord has risen upon you.*
>
> *For behold, darkness shall cover the earth, and thick darkness the peoples; but the Lord will arise upon you, and his glory will be seen upon you. And nations shall come to your light, and kings to the brightness of your rising.* (Isaiah 60:1-3)

This is a favorite passage to many preachers. Yet too many use these verses to describe the conditions of a current 'last days.' This is not a prophecy about the second coming of Jesus, it is a Messianic prophecy of Jesus' first coming. We have a promise that nations will come to the light of Jesus.

> *The Spirit of the Lord God is upon me, because the Lord has anointed me to bring good news to the poor; he has sent me to bind up the brokenhearted, to proclaim liberty to the captives, and the opening of the prison to those who are bound; to proclaim the year of the Lord's favor, and the day of vengeance of our God; to comfort all who mourn; to grant to those who mourn in Zion — to give them a beautiful headdress instead of ashes, the oil of gladness instead of mourning, the garment of praise instead of a faint spirit; that they may be called oaks of righteousness, the planting*

of the Lord, that he may be glorified. They shall build up the ancient ruins; they shall raise up the former devastations; they shall repair the ruined cities, the devastations of many generations. (Isaiah 61:1-4)

No one can deny this passage has new covenant applications, because Jesus quotes Isaiah and says it is fulfilled (Luke 4:18-21). Yet again, dispensationalists go the extra mile to separate a portion of this passage for their version of a future 'Great Tribulation' and their '1,000-year Millennium.' Since Jesus stopped reading after announcing the "Year of the Lord's favor" they presume the rest of the passage is separate and will be fulfilled in our future. This is poor exegesis and just plain bad theology. The "day of vengeance" came in the first century when the Temple and the city of Jerusalem were destroyed in the fall of 70 A.D. Jesus spoke often of this throughout the gospels and the Apostles did the same, in their letters. Just because Jesus did not read the entire prophecy of Isaiah does not mean He was giving it separate interpretations.

For as the earth brings forth its sprouts, and as a garden causes what is sown in it to sprout up, so the Lord God will cause righteousness and praise to sprout up before all the nations. (Isaiah 61:11)

If we misread the first few verses of Isaiah 61, we will also misinterpret this verse. When will the Lord bring about *"righteousness and praise"* in the nations? It did not happen under the old covenant. Again, only as we apply a Theological Interpretation of Scripture can we accurately see the full truth of this type of passages. This is our roots. Do not give them away!

Two problems

1. Dispensationalism

Since the church is not seen in any Old Testament passage, this must be about Israel in the millennial kingdom. Then, Jesus will come to them again and offer the kingdom (and the Spirit) and they will accept. This interpretation steals from the church and gives it to natural Israel in the future.

2. An Over-Realized New Covenant

This position holds that Christ fulfills all Old Testament promises. This view eliminates any Old Testament prophecies as being fulfilled in the church and accepts only promises, which are explicitly stated in the New Testament. This approach arrives at the same results as dispensationalism; the church is separated from its rich roots of Old Testament prophecy.

Discussion and Questions

1. Explain briefly the concepts of a "Christocentric" interpretation of Scripture and its relationship to a "Theological Interpretation of Scripture."

2. When Isaiah speaks of a *"covenant of peace"* and an *"everlasting covenant"* is there any other covenant, except the new covenant, established by Jesus, that He may have been prophesying about?

3. How does dispensationalism explain the many Messianic prophecies in the Old Testament?

4. What is an "An Over-Realized New Covenant" view of Old Testament prophecies?

Lesson 6
Releasing Creativity

Creativity in the church is often viewed as counter-productive. "We value tradition, we don't need new ideas; we must enforce the old ones." This kind of thinking is regressive, and the church finds itself unable to relate to its culture. Our faith, the Apostolic faith of the New Testament, never changes, but we need fresh imagination and gifting of the Holy Spirit, in order to know how to apply faith to our generation.

Our key to kingdom creativity is in the Holy Spirit. There are a variety of gifts we can receive from the Spirit and the Son. The problem begins when we teach the gifts of the Holy Spirit like they were limited in number. We teach the 9 gifts found in I Corinthians 12 but rarely teach the gifts found in Romans 12.

> *Now concerning spiritual gifts brothers, I do not want you to be uninformed.* (I Corinthians 12:1)

Teaching is a necessity. God's people need to be informed about the gifts of the Holy Spirit.

> *Now there are varieties of gifts, but the same Spirit; and there are varieties of service, but the same Lord; and there are varieties of activities, but it is the same God who empowers them all in everyone. To each is given the manifestation of the Spirit for the common good. For to one is given through the Spirit the utterance of wisdom, and to another the utterance of knowledge according to the same Spirit, to another faith by the same Spirit, to another gifts of healing by the one Spirit, to another the working of miracles,*

to another prophecy, to another the ability to distinguish between spirits, to another various kinds of tongues, to another the interpretation of tongues. All these are empowered by one and the same Spirit, who apportions to each one individually as he wills. (I Corinthians 12:4-11)

The Nine Gifts of I Corinthians 12

1. Word of Wisdom

2. Word of Knowledge

3. Faith

4. Gifts of Healing

5. Miracles

6. Prophecy

7. Discernment

8. Speaking in Tongues

9. Interpretation of Tongues

When people are exposed regularly to the gifts of the Spirit, they enter a world, where our spiritual and physical faculties are heightened. We feel better. We think clearer. Our imagination is filled with creative thoughts from God.

Having gifts that differ according to the grace given to us, let us use them: if prophecy, in proportion to our faith; if service, in our serving; the one who teaches, in his teaching; the one who exhorts, in his exhortation; the one who contributes, in generosity; the one who leads, with zeal; the one who does acts of mercy, with cheerfulness. (Romans 12:6-8)

1. Prophecy

2. Service

3. Teaching

4. Exhortation

5. Giving

6. Leadership

7. Acts of Mercy

Paul's list in Romans begins with prophecy, which is also listed in I Corinthians 12. The other six gifts are different. So, if we add the 6 to the 9, we arrive at 15 gifts. Are we done yet? No there are more.

> *Now you are the body of Christ and individually members of it. And God has appointed in the church first apostles, second prophets, third teachers, then miracles, then gifts of healing, helping, administrating, and various kinds of tongues.* (I Corinthians 12:27-28)

Here we see a repeat of many gifts already mentioned, but there is an additional one; administration. Therefore, we can add administration to our list, which makes the number of gifts 16. Are there more?

> *Therefore it says, "When he ascended on high he led a host of captives, and he gave gifts to men."* (Ephesians 4:8)

Notice that Paul says the Ascended Christ "*gave gifts to men*". It does not say 'offices'. It does not mean these gifts cannot be official 'offices' in the government of the church, but for now we need to recognize the text says only "gifts".

> *And he gave the apostles, the prophets, the evangelists, the shepherds and teachers, to equip the saints for the work of ministry, for*

building up the body of Christ, until we all attain to the unity of the faith and of the knowledge of the Son of God, to mature manhood to the measure of the stature of the fullness of Christ. (Ephesians 4:11-13)

Now we have a list of five gifts to the church. Three of them - apostles, prophets (if we include prophecy) and teachers - are on our list. We have two new ones to add, evangelists and pastors (or shepherds). Therefore, adding to our list of gifts we arrive at 18.

These five Ascension gifts are said to *"Equip the saints for the work of ministry"*. They are leaders who serve the church. They are responsible to see the church grow into the *"Fullness of Christ"*. In much of our history, we have limited the Ascension gifts to pastors, along with a few evangelists and teachers. Even with the church's acceptance of evangelists and teachers, most needed to go outside the local churches to fulfill their calling. Many evangelists began their own organizations and most called as teachers went into the academic world of Bible Schools and Seminaries. Being exposed regularly to all five of these Ascension gifts would benefit the local church.

Over the last generation God has released Apostles and Prophets back into the church. We have seen swings both good and bad in our attempt to get it right. One thing is for sure, God will continue to give these Ascension gifts, because the church needs them.

Are we seeing these 18 gifts used in the church? If not, why not? Over the years I have noticed that in traditional Pentecostal Churches, speaking in tongues with interpretation is valued, whereas in Charismatic Churches prophecy is the preferred gift. We tend to get in ruts and limit what God may want to do.

The kingdom of God is advancing and will fill the earth with the *"knowledge of the Lord as the waters cover the sea"*

(Isaiah 11:9). Knowledge can be given by gifts of the Holy Spirit.

Old Testament Gifts

> *The Lord said to Moses, "See, I have called by name Bezalel the son of Uri, son of Hur, of the tribe of Judah, and I have filled him with the Spirit of God, with ability and intelligence, design, with knowledge and all craftsmanship, to devise artistic designs, to work in gold, silver, and bronze, in cutting stones for setting, and in carving wood, to work in every craft. And behold, I have appointed with him Oholiab, the son of Ahisamach, of the tribe of Dan. And I have given to all able men ability, that they may make all that I have commanded you: the tent of meeting, and the ark of the testimony, and the mercy seat that is on it, and all the furnishings of the tent, the table and its utensils, and the pure lampstand with all its utensils, and the altar of incense, and the altar of burnt offering with all its utensils, and the basin and its stand, and the finely worked garments, the holy garments for Aaron the priest and the garments of his sons, for their service as priests, and the anointing oil and the fragrant incense for the Holy Place. According to all that I have commanded you, they shall do."* (Exodus 31:1-11)

Setting aside the argument that this is part of the old covenant of Moses, I find it amazing that God gave gifts of intelligence, design, cutting and setting of stones, carving and any gift needed to build the place of worship. Maybe we should bring people forward in church and pray for the gift of intelligence.

These are more than natural abilities. The list begins with "*I have filled him with the Spirit of God*". People have talents from birth, yet, when the Holy Spirit fills them, we can expect an increase of ability and creativity within these gifts.

We no longer need a physical temple to worship in; we are God's temple in the earth. The church has replaced the Temple as the connection point between earth and heaven. Yet, I believe we can receive gifts that result in better function, beauty, artistic creations, inventions and thousands of applications, to make our world a better place. Why should we settle for only a handful of gifts, when God wants to pour them out in abundance?

> *So that through the church the manifold wisdom of God might now be made known to the rulers and authorities in the heavenly places*. (Ephesians 3:10)

God's dream is to release His wisdom and demonstrate it to all creation. This is our destiny. The glorious church revealing our heavenly Father.

For several generations, certain sections of the church have slid into an attitude of 'anti-intellectualism.' Have we forgotten we are to love God with all our minds (Matthew 22:37)? Our minds cannot remain stagnant; we must increase our understanding of God through the Scripture. Allister McGrath in *The Passionate Intellect* says, "The discipleship of the mind is just as important as any other part of the process by which we grow in our faith and commitment… theology is a passion of the mind."[11]

We need true 'spiritual worship' and we need also stimulating 'intellectual worship.' I am convinced the reason many churches are losing members is because of the lack of intellectual pursuit of God. When we fail to grow mentally, our emotions gets stretched out of proper alignment. We need balance.

Allister McGrath again: "The heartbeat of the Christian faith lies in the sheer intellectual delight an excitement caused by the person of Jesus of Nazareth."[12]

Our world is changing quickly. Certain professions today will be eliminated, and others created. Artificial Intelligence is coming in levels only a few thought possible just a few years ago. Instead of complaining about the 'growing evil' in the world, why not be at the tables of creation and influence. Virtual Reality will affect far more than entertainment. It will transform everything it touches. Yet, where are those filled with the Spirit to help lead the church into this world-changing technology? Have we undervalued the work of the Holy Spirit?

J. Scott McElroy says: "There are signs that a sort of renaissance is rising, a Holy Spirit-initiated movement to integrate the arts and creativity into churches. This movement has the real potential to revive and rejuvenate our congregations, enhance our understanding of God and bring to the body of Christ closer to maturity."[13]

We need to release new levels of kingdom worship. The songs of the kingdom are largely unwritten. With new words will come new sounds of music, the sound of the kingdom. As we move into greater flows of worship, there will be outpourings of Holy Spirt creativity. Be ready. Keep open.

The church needs a release of Holy Spirit creativity. We expect too little. We dream too little. Let's change that!

Discussion and Questions

1. Why have so many in the church limited the gifts to the 9 we find in I Corinthians 12?

2. Should the 5 gifts in Ephesians 4 be interpreted as offices in the church, or gifts given to the church? What is the difference?

3. Are there gifts you have never seen manifest in the local church?

4. How can the church better release Holy Spirit creativity in the saints?

Footnotes
[11] Allister McGrath, *The Passionate Intellect*, IVP Books, Downers Grove, Illinois, page 19, 21

[12] Ibid.

[13] J. Scott McElroy, *Creative Church*, InterVarsity Press, Downers Grove, Illinois, page 14

Lesson 7
The Church and
Victorious Eschatology

When people use the biblical language of the kingdom, it is imperative that we support it with biblical understanding. Today we have those who use 'kingdom language' yet use it only in a 'popular' sense. Kingdom language is now acceptable, it is finally 'cool'. Nevertheless, without a biblically based kingdom eschatology, we will eventually grasp onto the newest wave of excitement and lose our vision for the kingdom. We need to begin with eschatology and then develop a vision consistent with the Scripture.

A few years ago, I read a book that outlined a great future for the nations. It was a wonderful read. The author wrote about 'cosmic redemption', about how God will restore everything lost in the fall. He made a good case against the division of secular from the sacred. He contended for the restoration of the arts and sciences. He spoke about the transforming of nations. Chapter after chapter I was reading about how God wants the earth restored and His glory filling the earth. Towards the end, though, his eschatology betrayed him and his readers. When reviewing the Lord's prayer in the gospel of Matthew he wrote:

"Jesus' request to his heavenly Father included charge to his disciples to be actively engaged in spreading the kingdom of God on earth. At the outset this sounds like an impossible task. But don't feel overwhelmed. One reason we instinctively flinch at the thought of such an undertaking is because Jesus said, 'Thy will be done,' He then said, 'As it is in heaven.' The result is that most people believe Jesus was calling the Church to create conditions on earth that reflect current conditions in heaven. Jesus did have heaven-like conditions in mind, but only in the distance future, when the present age has ended."[14]

So, after a great book, challenging the church to greater involvement in advancing the kingdom, he denies it will happen in the 'present age.' He did not state it, but I can only imagine there was a 'premillennial' conviction lurking behind his words. Most likely he believes we are now in the 'church age' and only after the return of Christ the 'kingdom age' will start. Therefore, we can work toward kingdom-age realities, but must also wait for the real thing. His conclusion - we are to work for cultural transformation, but not to expect much, until Jesus comes back. This type of thinking must be avoided. We are in the kingdom! The kingdom is advancing!

This is what happens when people have a 'kingdom vision' without a supporting 'kingdom eschatology.'

For those with 'kingdom vision' and 'kingdom eschatology', the task can be overwhelming. We live in the age of the kingdom and therefore the promises of the kingdom are for this age. The problem is, even when we accept the kingdom mandate, the job is so large, it seems impossible. Where do we begin? What is the process?

Please consider the following scenario. If everyone on earth matches your life, your morality and your spiritual life, would the world change? I believe the nations would be transformed overnight if this was true. Do you rob banks? Good. No more bank robberies, which would reduce insurance cost and reduce banking charges world-wide. Do you kill people using knives, guns or poison? Do you beat people to death with sticks? I hope not. If all the nations followed your example, all murders would stop immediately. This would save millions and millions of dollars on trials and prisons, and save families a lifetime of emotional pain. Do you appreciate God's creation and do what you can to keep it beautiful? If so, overnight millions of pounds of garbage on the streets across the nations would disappear. Do you get the point? **You are living a type of life right now, which, if duplicated, would transform the nations**. Everyone is important. Every ministry, no matter how small we think it is, is vital for the advancement of the kingdom of God.

The church needs a victorious view of the kingdom, if we are to take seriously the words of Jesus. He commanded His followers, and this includes us, to go and '*make disciples of the nations*" (Matthew 28:18-20). We also learn that this commission involves more than evangelism, because Jesus said we are to Baptize them and "*teaching them to observe all that I have commanded you.*"

What would occur if 90% of the world's population were saved today? Would Jesus return and say, "Well done church?" No, our task in the kingdom would continue. Teaching and bringing believers to maturity is a longer assignment than leading them into salvation. Therefore, it is imperative the church has a generational vision. We need to be involved in both evangelism and making disciples simultaneously.

Major Points of Victorious Kingdom View

1. The church is the new people of God, made up of Jews and Gentiles; by the cross of Jesus, the two groups are made into one new man.

2. The church and the kingdom occupy the same time. Both begin with the first coming of Jesus and continue without end. The Bible never teaches a 'church age'. We are the church and we live in the age of the kingdom. In the future, when the dead are raised, the kingdom of Christ is handed over to the Father.

3. The "*last days*" were the final days of the old covenant era. All the events of the last days occurred in the first century.

4. There is no "secret rapture" seven years before the second coming of Christ.

5. The "*great tribulation*" prophesied by Jesus occurred in the first century. It was the final covenantal judgment against unbelieving Israel. The major component was the destruction of Jerusalem and the temple.

6. The church presently fulfills promises made in the Old Testament, including prophesies concerning the kingdom of God and the new covenant. To properly interpret many Old Testament prophecies, we need a Christo-centric method of interpretation.

7. The church lives in the kingdom now. The kingdom of God will be victorious in time and space, on the earth. There is no need for a new temple in Jerusalem, neither will animal sacrifices ever be accepted by God. Nations will be made followers of Jesus, His enemies made a footstool, and the knowledge of the glory of God will cover the earth. The purposes of God include the renewal and transformation of the earth, not its destruction.

To understand the church is to understand the kingdom. There is no such thing as "We are leaving the age of the church and entering the age of the kingdom." What is occurring is that we are finally regaining previous truth given to the church about the kingdom. This is what happens when we *"to contend for the faith that was once for all delivered to the saints"* (Jude 3).

> *So, what do you think? With God on our side like this, how can we lose? If God didn't hesitate to put everything on the line for us, embracing our condition and exposing himself to the worst by sending his own Son, is there anything else he wouldn't gladly and freely do for us? And who would dare tangle with God by messing with one of God's chosen?*
> (Romans 8:31-33; The Message)

The Church is victorious. How can we lose? We cannot!

> *No, in all these things we are more than conquerors through him who loved us.*
> (Romans 8:37)

Apostle Paul does not say we are better at being 'conquerors', but we are more than conquerors. Why are we more than those using violence to conqueror? It is because our methods are superior. We win through love.

> *But thanks be to God, who in Christ always leads us in triumphal procession, and through us spreads the fragrance of the knowledge of him everywhere.* (II Corinthians 2:14)

> The Message says: *In the Messiah, in Christ, God leads us from place to place in one perpetual victory parade.*

This is a beautiful passage of the church's victory. Every single day of our lives in Christ, wherever we go, we are marching in "*one perpetual victory parade*".

Discussion and Questions

1. What are three things that you do regularly, that, if followed by a large majority, would cause a major transformation in the world?

2. Where does the concept of a 'Church Age' come from? What is the practical consequences of this view?

3. Have you seen those who use 'kingdom language', but their eschatology denies present and advancing kingdom on earth?

4. Are there more points that should be added to the "Major Points of Victorious Kingdom?"

5. Discuss the implication of being "more than conquerors?

Footnotes
[14] John Barber, *Earth Restored*, Christian Focus Publications, page 126

Lesson 8
The Communion of Saints

Fellowship with the saints is a neglected area of study. Why study something we do so naturally? Over the years, the time spent in fellowship with like-minded kingdom people has counted for the truly great moments in my life. Communion with the saints of God is foundational to His kingdom, because the 'kingdom of God is relationships'. I was intrigued when reading again the Apostles Creed, where it states, "I believe, in the communion of saints." Are we missing something in the kingdom? I believe this is not about those who are departed, but communion with the living. The understanding and experience of the 'communion of saints' is needed for the continued advancement of the kingdom.

The Apostles Creed

I believe in God, the Father almighty,
creator of heaven and earth.
I believe in Jesus Christ, God's only Son, our Lord,
who was conceived by the Holy Spirit,
born of the Virgin Mary,
suffered under Pontius Pilate,
was crucified, died, and was buried;
he descended to the dead.
On the third day he rose again;
he ascended into heaven,
he is seated at the right hand of the Father,
and he will come to judge the living and the dead.
I believe in the Holy Spirit,
the holy catholic Church,
the communion of saints,

the forgiveness of sins,
the resurrection of the body,
and the life everlasting. Amen.

What does this line about the 'communion of Saints' mean? Why was it included in a doctrinal statement of our early apostolic faith? For the saints of the first century it was a key to their walk with Jesus.

To enter the 'communion of saints' we first must establish our communion with God; and God in His triune person - Father, Son and Holy Spirit. There can be no real communion with one another before we have a relationship with God.

I John 1:3 Fellowship with the Father

That which we have seen and heard we proclaim also to you, so that you too may have fellowship with us; and indeed our fellowship is with the Father and with his Son Jesus Christ.

I Corinthians 1:9 Fellowship with the Son

God is faithful, by whom you were called into the fellowship of his Son, Jesus Christ our Lord.

II Corinthians 13:14 Fellowship with the Holy Spirit

The grace of the Lord Jesus Christ and the love of God and the fellowship of the Holy Spirit be with you all.

Our journey into this wonderful communion of saints begins with our fellowship with God the Father, Son and Holy Spirit. Without this vital living connection, all other human relationships and fellowships will fall short of what they could be.

And they devoted themselves to the apostles'
teaching and the fellowship, to the breaking of
bread and the prayers. (Acts 2:42)

When the Holy Spirit fell upon the people, they desired to
be with each other. The Holy Spirit leads us into this
communion of saints.

That which was from the beginning, which we
have heard, which we have seen with our
eyes, which we looked upon and have touched
with our hands, concerning the word of life—
the life was made manifest, and we have seen
it, and testify to it and proclaim to you the
eternal life, which was with the Father and
was made manifest to us— that which we have
seen and heard we proclaim also to you, so
that you too may have fellowship with us; and
indeed our fellowship is with the Father and
with his Son Jesus Christ. And we are writing
these things so that our joy may be complete.
This is the message we have heard from him
and proclaim to you, that God is light, and in
him is no darkness at all. If we say we have
fellowship with him while we walk in
darkness, we lie and do not practice the
truth. But if we walk in the light, as he is in
the light, we have fellowship with one another,
and the blood of Jesus his Son cleanses us
from all sin. (I John 1:1-7)

Pastor and author Douglas Wilson, quotes I John and
comments concerning the communion of saints.

"It is the communion of light. Through the
gospel, we have union with Christ. Because
we have union with the bridegroom, this
means that, of necessity, we have union with
the rest of the bride. The unity of the saints

flows from the head. The unity of the saints pervades the entire body of saints precisely because of their connection to the Lord. If we have fellowship with the Light, we have fellowship in the light."[15]

All communion begins with God. He is light. The communion of saints is the rich and deep connection we have with others, who also walk in the light.

As the church grows in revelation of the kingdom, the deeper the communion will be.

"But the dream of human communion can only come true when communion is first sought in God. And so in the Apostles' Creed, we remember the sacred story about the Father who created the world as a communion; the Son who came to restore the world to communion; and the Spirit who came to give this communion life."[16]

This is good, God "created the world as a communion." Humanity, since the cross, is not called to division. Yes, we have our separate 'nation groups', but the communion of saints surpasses patriotism and stands against nationalism.

The foundation of communion with the saints is not for personal enjoyment or enrichment, although that is the result; it is for the building up of our brother or sister in Christ. In the Heidelberg Catechism of 1563 this was made clear.

Q. What do you understand by the communion of saints?

A. First, that believers, all and everyone, as members of Christ have communion with him and share in all his treasures and gifts. Second, that everyone is duty-bound to use his gifts readily and cheerfully for the benefit and well-being of the other members.

The Christians living in the first decades after the Protestant Reformation saw the 'communion of saints' as their responsibility, so they can share the 'treasures and gifts' of Christ with those in His body; the church. How should we do this? We should do it readily and cheerfully. Apostle Paul wrote about this in his letter to the Romans.

For as in one body we have many members, and the members do not all have the same function, so we, though many, are one body in Christ, and individually members one of another. Having gifts that differ according to the grace given to us, let us use them. (Romans 12:4-6)

We have been given gifts. The purpose of gifts is for the benefit of others. Sharing what God has given us with others is vital to experiencing the 'communion of saints.'

If there is any encouragement in Christ, any comfort from love, any participation in the Spirit, any affection and sympathy, complete my joy by being of the same mind, having the same love, being in full accord and of one mind. Do nothing from selfish ambition or conceit, but in humility count others more significant than yourselves. Let each of you look not only to his own interests, but also to the interests of others. (Philippians 2:1-4)

The Message: *If you've gotten anything at all out of following Christ, if his love has made any difference in your life, if being in a community of the Spirit means anything to you, if you have a heart, if you care— then do me a favor: Agree with each other, love each other, be deep-spirited friends. Don't push your way to the front; don't sweet-talk your way to the top. Put yourself aside, and help* *others get ahead. Don't be obsessed with getting your own advantage. Forget yourselves long enough to lend a helping hand.*

In his letter to Philemon, Apostle Paul shares what this 'communion of saints' looks like.

Every time your name comes up in my prayers, I say, "Oh, thank you, God!" I keep hearing of the love and faith you have for the Master Jesus, which brims over to other believers. And I keep praying that this faith we hold in common keeps showing up in the good things we do, and that people recognize Christ in all of it. Friend, you have no idea how good your love makes me feel, doubly so when I see your hospitality to fellow believers. (Philemon 1:4-7)

And let us consider how to stir up one another to love and good works, 25 not neglecting to meet together, as is the habit of some, but encouraging one another, and all the more as you see the Day drawing near. (Hebrews 10:24-25)

The communion of saints means we are to "*stir up one another*", so we will be more loving and engaged in good works.

The author of Hebrews was writing only a few years before the '*Day of the Lord*' spoken of by Jesus and other Apostles. It was the judgment upon covenant breaking Israel, when the Temple and the city were destroyed. This was the "Day" drawing near. We should always meet together on a regular basis, but to miss church in Jerusalem during that time might have cost you and your family your life. Why? Because the Holy Spirit was reminding the people what was about to happen. I believe as the day got closer, there were more prophetic words, reminding the church of the signs Jesus gave (Matt. 24).

In our modern fast-paced culture, many rush to church and then hurry off to the next thing. We are missing a vital kingdom experience, when we are not engaging in the communion of saints. Do not wait for someone to share their gift with you, you share first. Experience the great reward of being together.

Communion of the saints is the cure for loneliness. It meets our basic need to connect with others on a spiritual level. Communion of saints is the remedy for many societal ills. It is badly needed in the church. The kingdom of God on earth must be more than a great vision - it must be our daily experience of the communion of saints.

When I was a pastor, I noticed over the years, that new people coming into the church, who did not make several friendships within the first few months, normally left the church. Our connection to the saints must be real. No believer is to walk out their faith alone. We need each other.

Many churches now have only one or two services a week, which is fine. Therefore, leadership needs to encourage the people to spend time in fellowship with one another outside scheduled services. We should not wait for 'church' to experience fellowship. Let us go deeper into this communion of saints.

Discussion and Questions

1. Have you heard many sermons on the 'communion of saints?'

2. Evangelicals have largely ignored the Historic Creeds of the church; why?

3. Discuss "As the church grows in revelation of the kingdom, the deeper the communion will be."

4. Discuss the meaning of the 'communion of light.'

5. What would the church look like, if we were as committed to 'fellowship' (communion of saints) as we are to the other aspects of Acts 2:42?

Footnotes

[15] Douglas Wilson, Blog & Mablog,
https://dougwils.com/books/apostles-creed-18-communion-saints.html
[16] Charles Erlandsan
http://www.patheos.com/blogs/giveusthisday/mean-communion-saints/#

Lesson 9
When the Mission is Accomplished - The Resurrection of the Dead

Everyone wants to know the future. When I die, will I live again? Will I be a puff of spiritual smoke for eternity? Or does God have something else in mind? The doctrine of the resurrection of the dead has been hijacked by numerous spurious teachings. The cure for bad doctrine is good doctrine. If the church had maintained a strong place for the 'resurrection of the dead' as part of their non-negotiable doctrines, I would like to think we would be better off today. But things are changing. The teaching of the kingdom is bringing balance back into the church. When we understand the kingdom then our task of unraveling other doctrines becomes easier. The doctrine of the resurrection of the dead is next to be realigned to better fit the biblical text and our understanding of God's advancing kingdom.

What happens when the mission of the church is over? The church is called to disciple the nations. We will not know exactly when a nation is discipled from God's viewpoint. Therefore, we do not know 'when' the resurrection of the dead will take place. What we do have, are guidelines for our mission and the Bible does say Jesus reigns from heaven 'until' the mission is complete.

What is the resurrection of the dead? For most of church history there has been acceptance of the future physical resurrection of the dead, until lately. We now have Christians denying any future resurrection of the dead or they define it in such a way as to make the historic doctrine of the church of no avail.

Four Views of the Resurrection of the Dead

1. Historic Christian View

In the future, at the end of the age, Jesus returns to earth and those 'in Christ' receive their resurrection bodies. This body is patterned after the resurrected body of Jesus. It has 'spiritual' aspects, while being a 'physical' body at the same time. This has been affirmed by the ancient Christian creeds.

Apostles' Creed - The last two lines

> I believe in the Holy Ghost; the holy catholic Church; the communion of saints; the forgiveness of sins; **the resurrection of the body**; and the life everlasting. Amen.

The Apostles' creed is the earliest statement of faith in the church. It represents the key doctrines established by the New Testament authors.

Nicene Creed - The last three lines

> We believe in one holy catholic and apostolic Church.
> We acknowledge one baptism for the forgiveness of sins.
> **We look for the resurrection of the dead**, and the life of the world to come. Amen.

The resurrection of the dead was the future hope for all believers.

Athanasian Creed - final few lines

> He ascended into heaven, He sits at the right hand of the Father, God Almighty, from whence He will come to judge the quick and the dead. **At His coming all men will rise again with their bodies** and shall give account for their own works.

Even if we disagree with the Historic position of the church, we must recognize that these creeds represent what the church believed since the earliest of times. Christians for centuries believed it was more than a spiritual resurrection - it was a 'resurrection of the body.'

2. Dispensationalism

Here is a statement about the resurrection from a dispensational viewpoint.

> "We believe that at death the spirits and souls of those who have trusted in the Lord Jesus Christ for salvation pass immediately into His presence and there remain in conscious bliss until the resurrection of the glorified body when Christ comes for His own, whereupon soul and body reunited shall be associated with him forever in glory; but the spirits and souls of the unbelieving remain after death conscious of condemnation and in misery until the final judgment of the great white throne at the close of the millennium, when soul and body reunited shall be cast into the lake of fire, not to be immediately annihilated, but to be punished with everlasting destruction from the presence of the Lord, and from the glory of his power."[17]

Dispensationalism differs from the Historic view in that it has a two-stage resurrection. The first resurrection is of all Christians at the rapture, and the second resurrection for unbelievers waits until the close of the 1,000-year millennium. Dispensationalism is a departure from the historic view of the church.

3. Full Preterism

Those advocates of a 'spiritual resurrection' at death, who say there is no future physical resurrection, are called

Full Preterists. There are differences of thought among Full Preterists, yet none would accept a future resurrection of the dead, in which our resurrection would be patterned after the resurrection of the body of Jesus. Here is a quote from Full preterist David Curtis.

> "This problem of joint ownership of atoms and molecules is a big problem. After death, various body particles returned to dust, reentered the food chain, got assimilated into plants, eaten by animals, and digested into countless other human bodies. At the resurrection, who gets which atoms and molecules back? As you can see, it can get quite complicated. Another thing that bothered me was why does God raise our dead decayed bodies, put them all back together just to change them into immortal spiritual bodies."[18]

I have read many articles by Full Preterists, on the resurrection, and many of them take this approach. Yet, for me, what is important is not the "How" of the resurrection, but "What does the Scripture say?" If we applied human logic to other doctrines, we would end up denying many truths found in the Bible. I have no answer as to how God will do what is impossible, but that is the nature of God; to do supernatural things. Does the Scripture teach the resurrection of the dead that is formed after the 'First-fruits' of Jesus' body? That is the question, not if it seems possible or not.

Curtis continues his Full Preterists view of the resurrection.

> "Was Christ physically resurrected? Yes! Absolutely, without a doubt. Since Christ's resurrection was physical, won't ours be? NO! Christ's actual resurrection was His going to Hades and coming back out. When he was

resurrected from Hades, He was raised into his original body, which was transformed into His heavenly form. This was done as a SIGN to the apostles that he had done what He had promised. The resurrection of Jesus' body verified for His disciples, the resurrection of the soul...Unless Jesus' body had been resurrected, His disciples would have had no assurance that His soul had been to Hades and had been resurrected. The physical resurrection of Christ was essential to verify the spiritual, to which it was tied. While the physical resurrection of our bodies would have no point, since we will not continue living on this planet, breathing earth's oxygen, and eating earth's food after we die physically."[19]

Is this your view of the resurrection of Jesus from the dead? When we begin our understanding with an erroneous view of Jesus' resurrection, it should be of no surprise that our resurrection from the dead will follow a similar view. Jesus was resurrected on the third day. He received a body that is both spiritual and physical. He enjoyed a fish dinner and He moved through physical objects and space like they did not exist. Jesus is the firstfruits of the type of body we all receive in the day of resurrection.

4. Partial Preterism

Those advocating that there is a future physical resurrection of the dead, in line with the Historic position, while affirming the past nature of events, such as the 'Great Tribulation,' 'appearing of anti-Christ,' and all the events of the 'last days', are Partial Preterists. Therefore, Partial Preterism endorses the ancient creeds of the church.

> But our citizenship is in heaven, and from it
> we await a Savior, the Lord Jesus Christ, who

will transform our lowly body to be like His glorious body, by the power that enables him even to subject all things to Himself. (Philippians 3:20-21)

The Message: *But there's far more to life for us. We're citizens of high heaven! We're waiting the arrival of the Savior, the Master, Jesus Christ, who will transform our earthy bodies into glorious bodies like his own. He'll make us beautiful and whole with the same powerful skill by which he is putting everything as it should be, under and around Him.*

The challenge for preterists is to determine if this is a 70 A.D. text, like we have in Matthew 10:23, Matthew 16:27, Matthew 24:27, II Thessalonians 2:1-8, James 5:7-9, II Peter 3:1-4 and other New Testament passages, or is it about a future coming, where 'earthly bodies' (like what we have now) will be transformed to be like Jesus' glorious body. The glorious body of Jesus is His post resurrection one. The only way this passage can be applied to 70 A.D. is to believe that all Christians living at that time received their resurrection bodies and were taken to heaven or they remain with us today. I accept this as one of the key passages, where the physical resurrection of our earthly bodies is described.

For as in Adam all die, so also in Christ shall all be made alive. But each in his own order: Christ the firstfruits, then at his coming those who belong to Christ. Then comes the end, when he delivers the kingdom to God the Father after destroying every rule and every authority and power. For he must reign until he has put all his enemies under his feet. The last enemy to be destroyed is death. (I Corinthians 15:22-26)

The context in this chapter is the resurrection of the dead. Apostle Paul concludes by comparing the first Adam with Christ. Adam brought death. Christ brings life. Paul states that Christ is the 'firstfruits.' Firstfruits of what? Christ is the firstfruits of a resurrected body. His body was transformed into a type of body never seen before. Those, like Lazarus, who came back to live in a normal body, eventually died. The resurrection body is eternal. At the final return of Christ, those 'in Christ' receive the same type of body as he received.

> *Truly, truly, I say to you, an hour is coming, and is now here, when the dead will hear the voice of the Son of God, and those who hear will live. For as the Father has life in himself, so he has granted the Son also to have life in himself. And he has given him authority to execute judgment, because he is the Son of Man. Do not marvel at this, for an hour is coming when all who are in the tombs will hear his voice and come out, those who have done good to the resurrection of life, and those who have done evil to the resurrection of judgment.* (John 5:25-29)

Here we have a two-stage resurrection, but not like the dispensational one. Jesus teaches that first we have a 'spiritual resurrection' and later a 'physical resurrection.' The latter is referring to a physical resurrection, as it says, "*all who are in the tombs will come out*". Yes, it goes against all common sense. How can "ALL" who are dead, come out. Nevertheless, unless convinced by Scripture my conviction is that there is yet a future bodily resurrection. This is the position of Partial Preterists.

N.T. Wright on the Resurrection
"Paul declares that "*flesh and blood cannot inherit God's kingdom*". He doesn't mean that physicality will be

abolished. "*Flesh and blood*" is a technical term for that which is corruptible, transient, heading for death. The contrast, again, is not between what we call *physical* and what we call *nonphysical*, but between corruptible physicality, on one hand, and incorruptible physicality, on the other."[20]

"Why will we be given new bodies? According to the early Christians, the purpose of this new body will be to rule wisely over God's new world. Forget those images about lounging around, playing harps. There will be work to do and we shall relish doing it. All the skills and talents we have put to God's service in this present life (perhaps also the interests and likings we gave up, because they conflicted with our vocation) will be enhanced, enabled and given back to us to be exercised for His glory. This is perhaps the most mysterious and least explored aspect of the resurrection life."[21]

Discussion and Questions

1. Discuss why dispensationalists separate the resurrection of the righteous and that of the unjust by 1000 years?

2. Discuss any other Full Preterist view of the resurrection of the dead.

3. Is it possible to maintain a 'partial preterist' eschatology and apply the bodily resurrection of the dead to the events in 70 A.D.? Why does it seem (there are no valid statistics) that many, who adopt partial preterism slide into full preterism over time? Is it the truth or is there a serious lack of teaching on the Historic position on the resurrection of the dead?

4. What are the practical applications of this doctrine?

5. Do you agree with N.T. Wright's view that our talents, skills and even interests not explored (life is just too short) will be given back enhanced in the resurrection of the dead?

Footnotes

[17] Dispensational Friends, Statement of Faith,
http://dispensationalfriends.org/statement.html

[18] David Curtis, The Resurrection of the Dead,
http://www.preteristarchive.com/Hyper/1999_curtis_resurrection.html

[19] Ibid.

[20] N.T. Wright, Surprised By Hope, Harper One, page, 156,
161

[21] Ibid.

Lesson 10
Kingdom First

But seek first the kingdom of God and his righteousness, and all these things will be added to you. (Matthew 6:33)

The Message: *Steep your life in God-reality, God-initiative, God-provisions. Don't worry about missing out. You'll find all your everyday human concerns will be met.*

Youngs Literal Translation (YLT): *But seek ye first the reign of God and His righteousness, and all these shall be added to you.*

Amplified Bible (AMP): *But first and most importantly seek (aim at, strive after) His kingdom and His righteousness [His way of doing and being right—the attitude and character of God], and all these things will be given to you also.*

Each of these versions brings out the force of Jesus' words. Jesus challenges us to seek the kingdom as a priority in everything we do. He wants to reign over our life. If these words bother us, we need to reexamine what it means for Jesus to be King of our lives. He is a King, who deeply loves His family. It should not be that difficult, but it is amazing how we have distorted, twisted, maligned and made religious, the simple command of Jesus.

Over the years the church has created several barricades to seeking first the kingdom. We shall explore several of them.

1. Misunderstanding Spirituality

Seeking first the kingdom of God does not mean we lose all sense of normal life. We are not called to center our life around religious activities. In history, monks moved to caves, so they would be able to focus only on God. Today churches fill the week's schedule with a multitude of services. Early in my Christian experience we had a robust church schedule. We started the week with a Sunday morning service, followed by a Sunday night service, then a Tuesday, Thursday and Friday services. On the days we were not in church we had at least 10 taped sermons to hear, every week.

When I was a teenager the general atmosphere in church was that the only true 'spiritual' people were pastors and missionaries. The rest were second-class Christians. We had to work, but we felt bad wasting so much time in such 'non-spiritual' pursuits. This type of separation of 'sacred' and 'secular' is not a 'kingdom first' mentality. True spirituality is walking in the Holy Spirit and living a Spirit-led life. When we walk in the Spirit, then driving a truck or leading worship is the same. In each pursuit we can be seeking first the kingdom of God.

2. Bad Eschatology

No one would make it a priority to seek a kingdom which is not available. The bad theology of the dispensational future kingdom has worked its way into modern culture. 'Until the kingdom comes' is an expression used by Christians and non-Christians alike. The kingdom is not an event in the future, but is in our experience of being connected to King Jesus. The damage done by separating the church from the kingdom, placing them in two different ages, is larger than we can imagine. Today, the message of our present life in the kingdom and the reign of King Jesus, is spreading to many nations. Over time this 'bad eschatology' will be forgotten.

3. Self-Centeredness

In recent times we have created yet another roadblock to seeking first the kingdom. It comes across as the 'purest' quest for the kingdom, but it misses what Jesus told us. There is a return to seeking the presence of God over everything else we do. If we can experience God in the truest intimacy, the highest level of fellowship, then, we will have reached Christian nirvana. Even though this is the essence of eternal life (John 17:3) we can easily go astray if taken in wrong way.

As an example, think of the consequences if the following scenario was true. You are single, no obligations to a spouse or children. Your uncle passed away and left you with millions of dollars. You quit work. You lock your door and decide to throw your entire being to 'seeking first the kingdom'. You have food delivered, so there is no reason to go out and run the risk of temptation or get distracted by the world. You have tremendous meetings with God, day after day. It is glorious. Nothing can compare. You now are one with God and with His kingdom. Are you sure? What is missing?

What is missing is the fact that the kingdom is about others, not just ourselves. Jesus said: "*As you treat one of the least of these, You have treated Me*" (Mt. 25:39). After the resurrection Jesus speaks to Peter. He asks, "*Peter, do you love me?*" When Peter answers in the positive, what was the response from Jesus? It is not, "Peter, withdraw from the other Apostles and disciples and live in a cave, so you can worship Me without any worldly distraction." No, Peter was to give his life in the service of others. Living a kingdom / new covenant lifestyle is about what we can give away, not what we can get. Of course, the more we get from God, the more we walk in the Spirit, the more we love and worship Jesus, the more we can give away.

Another self-centered approach is making our faith work to get things. The more things we possess; we interpret it has being 'more spiritual'. Our whole life is consumed with getting a larger car, better home, a more expensive watch, and it never ends. We are free to get all the 'things' in life we want, but do not confuse a steady gain of our net worth as 'seeking first the kingdom of God.'

How do we evaluate our love for Jesus and His Kingdom? Those in Pentecostal / Charismatic churches love to worship. We see voicing and singing our adoration for God as conceivably the highest thing we can do. It is in worship where we show how much we love God. As important as worship is, we must look at how Jesus responded to Peter.

> *When they had finished breakfast, Jesus said to Simon Peter, "Simon, son of John, do you love me more than these?" He said to him, "Yes, Lord; you know that I love you." He said to him, "Feed my lambs." He said to him a second time, "Simon, son of John, do you love me?" He said to him, "Yes, Lord; you know that I love you." He said to him, "Tend my sheep." He said to him the third time, "Simon, son of John, do you love me?" Peter was grieved because he said to him the third time, "Do you love me?" and he said to him, "Lord, you know everything; you know that I love you." Jesus said to him, "Feed my sheep."* (John 21:15-17)

Our love for Jesus can be measured on how we care for one another. We can stand for hours in church, singing great songs and telling Jesus how much we love Him, but unless it is revealed in a loving and caring nature for our fellow believers, we are falling short.

To define 'seeking first the kingdom' is not easy, because the kingdom cannot be defined in a sentence or two. If we use the closest thing to a New Testament definition - the one from Paul in Romans - we have only one aspect.

For the kingdom of God is not a matter of eating and drinking but of righteousness and peace and joy in the Holy Spirit. (Romans 14:17)

What prompted Paul to write these words? It is the climax of a chapter, where he is addressing practical problems in the church. In the church, people were dividing over if they should be eating only vegetables and if a certain day is better than another. Paul took what seems like previously asked questions and gave them guidelines to follow. Paul was giving them 'rules' to follow, because they needed them. I can only image, that at a certain point in laying out these rules, a Holy Spirit burst of energy came over him and he said to himself, "This walk with Jesus is not about a long list of rules", so he wrote, *"the kingdom of God is not a matter of eating and drinking but of righteousness and peace and joy in the Holy Spirit"* (Romans 14:17).

This is a great verse, the closest we have to a definition of the kingdom in Scripture. Yet, if we are to understand the kingdom of God, we must go beyond one verse. This verse tells us nothing about how the cross and resurrection of Jesus brought about the kingdom. In fact, it says nothing about Jesus at all. It tells us nothing of the explosive growth the kingdom will have. We cannot latch on to one verse and think it explains everything we need to know about any Scriptural topic. This leads to narrow-mildness and an unteachable spirit.

To summarize what it means to seek first God's kingdom is difficult, if not impossible. It covers so much territory and over a life time we will grow in what it means. Here is a beginning example of how we might begin to understand the meaning of what Jesus asked of us.

Seeking First the Kingdom of God

1. In order that we seek first the kingdom of God, we must know what the kingdom is.

Therefore, a study of biblical eschatology is needed, to see how the story of the Messianic reign of Jesus moves from the Old Testament to His incarnation in the first century. False assumptions concerning God's kingdom open the door for false views of spirituality.

2. In order that we seek first the kingdom of God, we must be born again into the kingdom (John 3:3).

3. In order that we seek first the kingdom of God, we must pursue the heart of God (John 4:21-24).

4. In order that we seek first the kingdom of God, we must love one another as Jesus loves us; this is the essence of the Law of Christ (John 13:34).

5. In order that we seek first the kingdom of God, we must develop a deep life in the Holy Spirit (Romans 14:17).

6. In order that we seek first the kingdom of God, we must embrace the rich root of the Hebrew prophets (Romans 11:17).

7. In order that we seek first the kingdom of God, we must avoid the many false and religious notions and engage both the Holy Spirit and the Scriptures, to guide our pursuit of the kingdom (Matthew 6:33).

Are we pursuing those areas, which add to and advance the kingdom of God on earth? Have we given our lives totally to King Jesus, to reign over us? Since we are told to seek first the kingdom, then, it all begins with the King of the kingdom; Jesus our Lord.

Discussion and Questions

1. What barriers have you experienced in seeking first the kingdom of God?

2. Discuss the problems in taking one verse and creating a complete theology out of it.

3. What does it mean to you, to "Seek first the kingdom of God"?

Books by Stan Newton

Glorious Kingdom
A Handbook of Partial Preterist Eschatology

Glorious Kingdom is a comprehensive book on eschatology; kingdom eschatology. In this book Stan Newton takes on dispensational eschatology, which is the position of many evangelicals and lays a foundation from Scripture for a different view. *Glorious Kingdom* covers all major aspects of eschatology with special emphasis on interpreting the prophetic New Testament passages from the viewpoint of the kingdom of God. The kingdom was established by Jesus in the first century. This book will help those seeking biblical answers to tough questions on eschatology.

Glorious Covenant
Our Journey Toward Better Covenant Theology

God is a God of covenants. Christians have a covenant. With these two basic foundations Stan Newton compares contemporary views of covenant. He examines Dispensationalism, Covenant Theology and New Covenant Theology. *Glorious Covenant* finds the fault lines of each position and then through Scriptural discovery argues for a fourth view - Better Covenant Theology. Sadly, many Christians are only vaguely aware of this glorious covenant. How followers of Jesus understand covenant is extremely important and *Glorious Covenant* removes the confusion and presents a clear view of the New Covenant we have in Christ.

Breakfast at Tel Aviv
A Conversation about Israel
Theological Fiction

Shane recently graduated from a Pentecostal Bible school. His future was secure within his denomination except one very large adjustment; he changed his theology. After finishing seminary, he moves back near his hometown church and former pastor, to begin his ministry. Pastor George is waiting for answers.

Over coffee the question is asked, "Shane, you have not abandoned Israel, have you?"

Breakfast in Tel-Aviv is the story of Pastor Shane and Pastor George as they share their positions on Israel. Emotions are high as they regularly discuss their views. Their discussions lead to a trip to Israel and over breakfast all is resolved; or is it?

Kingdom Communion

Kingdom Communion is written with the conviction that we are missing a great opportunity. If we continually see communion as 'not that important', our worship services will fail to make the kingdom transition I believe God is looking for. A revelation of Christ and His advancing kingdom affects every doctrine, and this includes the Lord's Supper. When the church celebrates communion like a wedding we will experience drinking the fourth cup with King Jesus.

All Books are Available on Amazon in Paperback or Kindle Edition

Kingdom Missions
The Ministry of Stan and Virginia Newton

We are singularly focused on teaching and demonstrating the Gospel of the Kingdom as taught in Stan's book, *Glorious Kingdom*. Through Seminars / Bible Schools / Churches we present the view of Christ's present and advancing Kingdom. Stan is available for speaking engagements in your church.

Virginia works in teaching English using a biblical curriculum and in literacy, where she helps develop workbooks to teach people to read.

We need your help in taking this message to the nations. You can E-mail us at svnewton@hotmail.com or become a friend on Facebook.

To send letters or financial gifts please mail to:

Kingdom Missions

PO Box 948

Seattle, WA. 98111

Also, give using PayPal. E-Mail for PayPal is: stannewton@live.com.

Made in the USA
San Bernardino, CA
25 June 2018